THE GUIDING P

One simple truth that reveals the miracle of your life

www.TheGuidingPrinciple.com

ABOUT THE AUTHOR

Davide De Angelis was born in London, England. He is a graphic designer, writer, shaman, artist… dad and vegan.

Davide's articles, audios and talks regularly attract a worldwide audience of over 40,000 people, and his wild and wonderful sci-fi novel, **The Seed** mysteriously became a cult classic in Russia of all places!

As an award winning designer and art director, he has worked for some of the most innovative companies and people in the world, including Apple, Virgin, Sony and the iconic David Bowie. His work is renowned for its radically experimental and beautiful ways of using language and images to communicate ideas. To connect with his design, art and creative projects visit: **www.DesignShaman.net**

Bowie describes Davide's work as "potent visual alchemy"

With a deep passion for delving into the mysteries of life and a heart-felt desire to help others express their fullest potential, Davide has spent over twenty five years studying the dynamics of Creative Expression, Shamanism, Self-Enquiry, Yoga, Coaching and a plethora of 'Personal Development' systems.

Alongside his work in design, art and multimedia, Davide has established an international reputation in the fields of Personal Development and Creativity Training, devising and facilitating workshops, learning programs and retreats. His unique combination of skills and experience gives him a totally unique viewpoint on what enables us to live extraordinary lives.

Central to everything he does is a sense of play, adventure and surprise.

GRATITUDE

Although I'm named as the author, this book is a celebration of many people. Amongst all the seemingly infinite interconnections and dynamics leading to this material, there is one person above all that has made this book possible: **Esther De Angelis.**

Not only is she my wife, soul partner and a gifted teacher, she is also the one who held the space for me to write this book. She is the one who sat talking ideas through with me, testing absolutely everything. Her creativity, profound desire for the truth and power to help people live joyfully and passionately is alive in this material. Her courage, amazing sense of wonder and her feminine wisdom guided, inspired and consistently opened me to new possibilities.

Esther, I love you deeply.

I invite you to connect with her:
www.EstherDeAngelis.com

I would like to give abundant thanks and respect to icon, legend, creative innovator... genius, David Bowie for believing in my designs, art and ideas and vitalising my own creative rebellion.

No need to say more:
www.DavidBowie.com

I would also like to give abundant thanks and blessings to my great friend, **Damien Senn**. Also a gifted teacher, his friendship, generosity, wise council and spirit of adventure have been instrumental to my journey and the creation of this book.

I invite you to connect with him:
www.DamienSenn.com

Published by Guiding Principle Publishing 2010/2013

ISBN   978-0-9565437-0-7

To discover more about 'The Guiding Principle' and related talks, podcasts, workshops, vision quests and retreats visit:

www.TheGuidingPrinciple.com

For Davide's graphic design, art and creative projects visit:

www.DesignShaman.net

To connect with Davide on Twitter:

@davidedeangelis

The Guiding Principle, Edited by Esther De Angelis

Cover artwork by Davide De Angelis

Photograph of Author by Esther De Angelis

Chapter heading artworks by Davide De Angelis

Abundant thanks to the super creative Rebecca Elliott for her wisdom and valuable feedback on the material.

Abundant thanks to the incredible Lunah Silver.

CONTENTS

"Treat every problem, every setback and every obstacle as sacred because they carry the seeds of your greatness."

Davide De Angelis

RE:VITALISED

I'm walking along the beach, hand in hand with my little daughter, Solaria. She is two years and two months. It's a beautiful day in early March. It is cold yet infused with the promise of spring.

As we toddle along together, the sun shines brightly. The small vestige of warmth it radiates seems to completely envelope us, as if it understands just how welcome it is.

We pause and look out to sea, watching sunbeams dancing across the waves.

Solaria suddenly points to the sun with incredible excitement.

"Sun!" She shouts, "Look Sun!"

She is new to language and appears to relish each word she speaks in a way that makes them truly precious.

Her next words heal me like an elixir, illuminating my soul.

"Daddy, sun speak to water.... sun speaking water."

I feel her tiny had clutching mine, sunlight as flesh. I feel the sun laughing its vast wisdom into my mind.

I know my little daughter is right. The sun is speaking to the water and the water speaks back to the sun. Beautiful and undeniable when so innocently pointed to.

The electromagnetic field in your brain is within the sun's electromagnetic field. This electromagnetic field permeates the entire solar system. Is it really such a leap to consider that the sun could sense everything that's going on in our brains, in our minds?

It's later, I'm walking through town watching countless people going about their business, seemingly completely unaware of the astonishing interconnectedness that grants them awareness – the astonishing miracle constantly at their fingertips - the message contained in The Guiding Principle is revitalised. It desires a new adventure.

In its short life this little book has managed to reach a lot of people.

Born as a physical book back in April 2010, after the launch party complete with drums and dancers, it languished mostly unnoticed on Amazon and gathered dust in a few bookstores for the first year of its life. Then through word of mouth and ghost-whispers, it ventured a little further into the world.

It wasn't until early 2012 when its digital siblings began to circulate that it quickly reached a much larger audience. Suddenly I started to receive emails asking me questions. Suddenly some people didn't like what I had to say and went out of their way to tell me so. Some thought it was science fiction or written by someone on LSD, while others wept with joy and recognition.

Now it had a life…

The Guiding Principle is no longer a book per se. It's a child of its time: a shape-shifter: a dynamic conversation rendered across print, ebook, sound, video… and art.

Regardless of whether you end up loving or hating it, or remain completely indifferent, you are now part of its ongoing creation. Amusingly, even people who buy it online and never read it effect the amount of people it reaches.

Pulsing at the epicentre of The Guiding Principle is a very simple invitation: an invitation to take a closer, more intimate look at your life: an intimate look at what you have taken to be true about who you are and what's true about life.

In The Guiding Principle I offer many exotic viewpoints for you to explore. Importantly none of these are fixed. Everything is open and ripe: transformation is the nature of every imaginable viewpoint.

I'm not telling you what to believe or trying to impart some new form of meditation practice. I'm not asking you to try and stop thinking, still your mind or imagine that you don't exist.

In the text I use words such as God, Nature, Consciousness and Presence, stating clearly that they are all interchangeable.

The Guiding Principle in all its forms is inviting you to see that the generally accepted reality – the way of things – is nothing more than provisional.

The Guiding Principle is a disruption of the story of separation and the constant soundtrack of anxiety that accompanies our lives.

It is proposing that the origin of our emotional sickness – and indeed all dysfunctional behaviour – emanates from the belief that we are these flimsy, ephemeral personalities: wispy, neurotic, wounded little gods bleeding their false realities over everything.

They came into being through no will of their own, possessing no capacity to see the magnificence that grants them existence. These little sirens drown in their own illusions as soon as our impulse to enquire grows strong enough to silence their song.

Mostly they don't sink easily though. Their passing can be turbulent, painful and complicated as they thrash around desperately trying to survive. Yet after they're gone we see that they were nothing more than astonishingly beautiful patterns appearing on the screen of Consciousness.

I predict with confidence that if you look closely and honestly you will discover that you are infinitely greater than what you call 'me' or 'self'.

Provocatively, The Guiding Principle is inviting you to see that your attention has been transfixed on one of these little personalities, unaware of who you really are and what's possible.

It is proposing that when the viewpoint or perspective of the knotted, afraid and uncomfortable little personality is questioned – really questioned with a desire to discover something new - you become potentialised.

From my own experience, and from the many other people I've come into contact with as a result of sharing this material, taking a closer look can completely transform a person's orientation to life. A willingness to question the reality that you have been prescribed ignites something in Nature: it ignites something in YOU.

When you become even momentarily open to a beautiful and creative viewpoint, it appears that Life or Consciousness loves this and readily provides the context and content in which you are able to freely create things... perhaps anything.

Maybe this potentiality, the possibility of radical transformation, is implicit in us all. It appears that just an instant of insight is fecund enough to fertilise a new person with new goals and values. The old persona is jettisoned, like the spent fuel tank of a rocket leaving the grasp of Earth's gravity.

From a 'higher' perspective, no longer pulled down by old stories and limitations, we can see the bigger picture. We can see our place in the scheme of things.

Going back to the Sun speaking to the water, I believe that our systematic disconnection from a reality that is vitally alive, responsive and completely interconnected and interdependent causes us to be afraid and deeply suspicious of life. We spend our time trying to protect ourselves from the 'threat' of life. Perhaps this is why so many grow old instead of ripe.

When we cannot see how incredibly porous the boundaries which appear to separate us actually are, we feel alone and isolated. Ask yourself if it's really possible to be totally separate, yet still be able to sense and feel and empathise with other people and living organisms.

The Guiding Principle gives you guidance and pointers on how to make your investigation. It never tells you what to think or experience. It sets the scene for your own enquiry.

Along the way you may discover that what you have taken to be true about life and the world is based on a series of assumptions. You may notice that the critical decisions that affect the shape of your life (and possibly the lives of everything) are made under conditions that practically guarantee discomfort. Through noticing what's happening, the possibility to create something new – something that works – is brought to life for you.

Perhaps you will start to notice in your own life how true power, which is effortless, slips past unnoticed and unused because force and struggle are incredibly visceral and easily capture your attention. With practice, it's possible to catch yourself trying to force things and instead open and soften to receive power.

As your enquiry deepens, you will stop wasting time searching for the 'truth'. You will see that truth, or what appears as a truth, reveals itself effortlessly.

You will most likely stop looking for a way out of your life. Instead you will see that your life is the very material from which you can create more or less anything.

We live in a culture where the miraculous invisibly glides past, and the unimaginable power at our disposal sits untapped. Our systems are built upon the forfeited pleasure and vital energy of the masses. Don't be surprised to find yourself taking a stand for a far more beautiful and loving paradigm and taking action – however small - to help it manifest.

We can easily see that small children are naturally connected to a unified reality. We gradually 'learn' how to forget this and so enter a restrictive world which functions by virtue of us staying afraid and asleep.

For way too long we have been trapped in a linear tunnel: more or less everything is a slave to convention.

I feel it's time for us to explore the 'impossible', because a life in service to what we're told is possible sends us back to providence unopened.

So I invite you to arrive at this material as you would arrive at a conversation that has the potential to open your heart and mind.

Use The Guiding Principle to bring your life to Life.

Start your investigation now.

You are beautiful beyond words.

Your life is made of the same stuff as miracles.

Davide
April 2013

NO WAY OUT

In the rain-drenched English Springtime of my forty-fourth year on Earth, life became intolerable. Most of the things that normally worked or appeared to work, systematically fell apart. Over the years I'd had my share of crises, but this was fundamentally different. The disruption to my world circumstances was totally overshadowed by a great sorrow. Darkness flooded from deep within my being.

At times this sorrow became so immense, that it seemed Nature Herself was mourning some irreplaceable loss. My heart was breaking for everything that unwittingly found itself manifest. I felt such sorrow bursting from everything. Even the sight of a dog playing, a car, a child laughing or a cloud hovering in a blue sky, broke my heart to the point where I had to avert my gaze. I would close my eyes and still experience the same sorrow in the endless repetitions playing out in my mind. The misery was inescapable and engulfed my entire reality. It was like being unravelled or prized away from the root of existence, and I spent weeks awash with a soul-numbing sense of complete futility.

I felt my heart and my internal organs being infused with this terrible darkness. And the hypochondriac in my nature became convinced that a terminal illness was eating me away from inside.

The darkness and utter futility roaming my being was often nudged aside by a deep hatred of life and everything it appeared to represent or mean. I was confronted with the utter stupidity and ridiculousness of the world. I saw life as a completely disinterested and ultimately malignant joke, with nothing orchestrating it and nothing to heal our broken hearts at the end. It truly seemed irresolvable.

This utterly dreadful state was further amplified by the fact that after more than twenty years of intense spiritual practice - learning from some of the world's most gifted Teachers and Shamans - I understood nothing of value. Years of working in the field of personal development and transformation, years of intense research and experience had boiled down to zero. It seemed that not a single thing that I had mastered could free me from the all-encompassing cloak of misery.

As my life faltered and crumbled around my ears, the vitality-draining shadow of shame also took possession of my mind. It scattered my sense of reason like an angry poltergeist, smashing any possibility of hope. During this time I saw clearly how shame, perhaps the lowest vibration of all, eats away at our will and drives us to become someone we can't stand the sight of.

Despite my utter disenchantment, the compulsion to lie about how I was doing and make it look good was powerful. Simultaneously though, my words took on a hollow, empty ring that I could clearly hear even if others appeared not to. And I noticed that some of the more sensitive people I encountered hovered around my false tones and seemed to pay close attention to my eyes, as if they were searching for the correct answers.

Shame is the maker of the masks we wear to cover up the truth. We are taught to be ashamed and it sticks like glue: it's hard unrewarding work and doesn't come naturally. We rarely give anyone – not even those closest to us – the gift of seeing our raw unmasked self in all its beautiful, uncomfortable truth. Shame convinces us that the truth is wrong when in fact it's our reconnection to the source of power. But ironically from within the cloud of shame it's difficult to see this. We have no idea that way down in the dirt of existence, we can discover our miraculous nature waiting to embrace us.

Eventually the eroding effect of self-loathing wore away all pretence. As the truth seeped through the cracks in my life it became increasingly difficult to maintain superficial appearances.

The knee jerk reaction to cover the truth with stories designed to maintain a false identity dissolved.

Most of us have witnessed this in people that have hit rock bottom. The dominion of shame finally collapses and they are right there in the moment stripped bare of any pretence. They come right out with what's on their mind and to hell with what anyone may think.

This is a reason why we stop and stare in utter fascination. No matter what words come out, we sense the possibility of how astonishing we could be and how free we could be, beneath the façade of being reasonable. Shame blights the miraculous in us. Free of shame there is no telling what may happen – no telling what amazing people we may become. But from such close proximity, the joke is that we can't see this. I certainly couldn't see it and although my words no longer carried the added burden of lies, to me they still sounded like a death rattle in my throat.

That death rattle had been ringing in my ears for weeks as the misery continued. The possibility of suicide had entered my mind again and again. Despite being dismally unpleasant for those left in its wake, it seemed like a possible way out. That was, until a thought suddenly arose, that death might not actually put an end to the sorrow that appeared to pervade everything. This grim thought injected doubt into the possibility of it ever ending: this was utterly terrifying. I had arrived at the place I feared more than anything else. A place where there is no God and not an ounce of joy: a place with no conceivable way out.

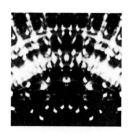

THE DISCOVERY

One bleak day whilst walking in hopeless circles around the woods close to my home, torrential rain poured from the sky like a curse. A swell of immense anger and resentment flooded to the surface. Everything seemed hostile. To my astonishment I heard myself screaming my hate for God. I was shocked because any belief in a divine presence had completely disappeared.

I felt all my vitality draining away and my heart pounded as if it would smash right through my chest. A searing pain gripped my heart and I gasped for breath. It flashed through my mind that I was about to die. What had become of my life would end here. There was tremendous fear. And standing in the midst of that fear I had the overwhelming urge to be buried in the earth: to return to the earth. And without giving it any consideration, I dropped to my knees and gouged away great clods of mud with my hands. Racked with pain, pouring with sweat and utterly exhausted, I collapsed facedown in the mud: the intense sorrow bursting out of the earth beneath my body.

As impossible as it felt, if there was a God moving my mind and body, I wanted to punish it for putting me in this wretched world full of unhappiness and death.

Then, without warning, as I lay face down covered in mud, a huge cracking sound came from deep within my chest. It sounded like someone snapping a large stick. An equally loud cracking sound in my throat immediately followed. The two sounds happened so quickly and so unexpectedly that all thought instantly ceased. There were suddenly no thoughts and there was no time passing; yet I was still vividly aware.

Without thought, a realisation swept through this spaciousness like an intelligent wind. It carried a message that I was already acting out the punishment of God through my self-obsession. And believing that I was separate from God or Nature caused the suffering.

Still without a single thought, this intelligent wind carried a deeper realisation that appeared to trigger a chain reaction. It began with seeing that I could only be an expression or aspect of something utterly miraculous. This was always the case whether I believed it or not: anything else was impossible. Then came the absolute knowing that God, Nature – The Miraculous - was this very experience; it was all I could ever know.

And finally, carried in on the wind of pure intelligence, came the realisation that the deep sorrow I had pushed away like poison was also God: the elixir.

Suddenly without the veil of thoughts there was just the birthing of experiences into the boundless, awake receptor of every possible experience: they existed simultaneously in perfect harmony.

As this realisation seeped into my being, and without knowing how, I started to journey into the sorrow and despair. And as I travelled deeper it began to open out and soften. In that instant it felt as if I was finally seeing something that I'd lived my entire life without noticing.

I had the strong feeling that I was staring through the illusion of time and witnessing something that had been so obvious yet completely hidden.

Out of pure, thoughtless space arose the experience of being a small child and suddenly feeling separate, believing myself to be separate from God. Through those innocent eyes I saw what appeared to be a world where people we love can die and animals we love can die. I saw that I could die and that there was wickedness and fear. And although I noticed these frightening qualities in the world I somehow felt that they were also part of me too: this was the birth of a belief that there was something fundamentally wrong with both the world and me. Looking through the veil of separation I saw a world to be afraid of. I desired to go back to the simple wonder and unity that existed before language and self-awareness.

I was witnessing anger and fear appearing in the mind of a small child – the anger and fear of feeling removed from unconditional love and placed in a realm of separation and limitation. I understood how much that irrational, innocent child wanted to lash out at whatever or whoever had placed him in this uncomfortable and alien world.

With this seeing came the realisation that this apparent 'loss of unity' sits incubating within most of us. It's never noticed that the discomfort simmering away beneath the surface is a fundamental misperception that we have lost our connection to Nature, The Miraculous. As a result we are constantly seeking relief from the discomfort caused by this perceived loss of unity.

I was astonished to see that all the pain I'd caused myself and others was a futile attempt to reconcile a loss which had in fact never happened - could never happen.

And yet the belief that there is such a thing as separation from God, the Divine, Unity – whatever you choose to call it – projects a kind of virtual-self into a virtual world of threat, pain and struggle to survive: each one mirroring back and amplifying the discomfort of separation. Sadly, for many people, this hall of mirrors eventually reflects back a kind of hell.

As I continued to journey into the sorrow, it flowered. All the chaos and turmoil it had originally appeared to contain stopped and was replaced by a beautiful, loving totality or presence.

My thoughts were suddenly rebooted by another very loud crack from inside my head. It sounded like my skull was being snapped back into place and what followed was simply total and utter comfort with life. Absolutely nothing was being resisted. And in this open, expansive acceptance it was completely obvious that nothing can ever be separate from the Divine, from God. It was seen that I wasn't creating this experience and I had never created any experience, yet experience happened.

It was also obvious that God or Nature is so intimate with us that She will wait forever in a pit of sorrow for us to discover our truth: love will wait forever in hate, good will wait forever in what we perceive as evil, until we find our truth.

Face down in the mud there was elation at the simple fact that I was alive at all: a simple felt moment of immediate presence followed by another and another…the mind and body aware of the intelligence that grants them life.

FREEDOM

I slowly liberated myself from the makeshift grave of mud and made my way home marvelling at the wonder of life. I'd had what may be called powerful spiritual experiences in the past but this was completely different: it was like the world, including this experience called Davide, was being directly registered in consciousness. It was like you could take my eyes away and there would still be sight or take my body away and there would still be experiencing. However it wasn't a form of detachment that is sometimes spoken about in spiritual teachings: it was a direct intimacy. It didn't actually have the glowing qualities of a spiritual experience at all; instead it offered pure, unveiled clarity.

Importantly, what I had previously thought to be me was actually just life arising in an unimaginably vast, joyful freedom: the vast, joyful freedom was always present and could never be destroyed or diminished: this was my true identity.

Walking along the road I wondered why people were staring and suddenly remembered that I was completely caked in mud and leaves. I must have looked pretty strange but I didn't care. I even bumped into a neighbour who thought I had fallen over. She couldn't help herself and started laughing and it sounded so good.

For several days after, life took on an exquisite quality and I understood that this is in fact our natural state of being. Even my life appearing not to work was exquisite. The serious stuff was seen not to be serious. I was experiencing what it was like to be natural and walk this beautiful Earth and know it totally and intimately as my home.

Beliefs and aspects of my personality that had previously caused me discomfort appeared to dissolve into a loving energy that was moving me through time. I noticed that this energy was in fact moving and shaping everything. It was the same wind of pure intelligence that I had encountered whilst face down in the mud. It was a presence that could move through timeless stillness. And it was simply vitally alive to its own nature. I instantly knew this was the guiding aspect of Nature.

I was surprised because I had always assumed that truth was a kind of peace, but in fact I saw it was unbridled, aliveness in any form of experience. Life lived the natural way was without resistance to aliveness as it arose moment to moment.

Physical characteristics that had caused me hidden shame no longer needed to be hidden. I understood on a deep level that only I could see them. Instead, seeing them as miracles manifest in flesh, made life taste like nectar. Life, without the burden of shame caresses instead of slaps.

Beyond any intellectual notion, I understood that we only see our beliefs looking back at us when we place our gaze upon someone else. So there was never anyone looking at me. In reality there is no judgement by or of others. All judgement and self-punishment is the result of seeing something that isn't actually there. In the absence of the illusion that we are incomplete we are all beautiful and perfect as we are. As strange as it may seem, every single person is doing exactly the right thing. The monk is doing exactly the right thing and the murderer is doing exactly the right thing. The successes and the failures are all doing exactly the right thing.

My mind now seemed to reflect or serve 'Being' or 'Nature', rather than trying to control it with false projections. The projections still happened but they no longer contained any power. I was able to perceive what was actually animating life: this was the seeing of what I have come to term as **The Guiding Principle**. It was still so new and still so fresh that I felt as if I was being gifted a whole new vocabulary of existence. Paradoxically though, in the same way that we don't need language to explain love, The Guiding Principle doesn't need language or thoughts to be perfectly understood.

As a spell is broken in fairy tales, once I saw that the projections of fear and suffering could only arise in my experience and that my direct experience was always God, there was no longer a rejection of them.

And without the reflex of rejection they were left to be what they were. As difficult as it may be for most of us to accept, when it is seen that pain and unhappiness bear the signature of God then God becomes alive in pain: the beliefs and stories that surround the pain or unhappiness fall away and we are just left with life unfolding from moment to moment. In this vibrant aliveness pain may come or stay without judgement. And without judgement pain mysteriously appears to give rise to the possibility of touching our deepest truth.

ALIVE INTELLIGENCE

Over the course of time the vibrant and very dramatic exquisiteness gently diminished. Leaving behind in its wake a very alive intelligence that effortlessly moved and shaped everything. This 'alive intelligence' is in fact the ordinary undercurrent of life that we all share, except its mostly not recognised as the wonder it actually is.

As time passed, I was also left with an intense awareness of movements in my mind and body. It felt as if my entire being was reorganising itself around a different energetic alchemy. It was like consciousness cleansing itself, letting go of its exclusive identification with all the stories that kept the previous me glued together: the 'old me' had died and fallen apart in the mud and worms. I didn't actually know what had returned, but the glaring absence of sorrow and discomfort gave the impression of being renewed in some way.

Interestingly I was able to observe how the deeply engrained habit of anxiousness moved to re-establish itself in my mind. It was like watching a fox trying to sneak into a hen house, however there was no movement or desire to try and stop this happening. It mysteriously arose from nowhere and went nowhere.

It became totally clear that I had been so engrossed in not seeing my own true nature that I had never fully seen just how uncomfortable practically everyone was in this world: in other words, how unwelcome most of us feel. Of course when we see people suffering in war zones or children starving in parched deserts it's overwhelmingly obvious. When we see stress and depression it's obvious. But this was everywhere. It was in the most ordinary of circumstances, where on the surface everything looked perfectly fine.

Seeing this so clearly lit a deep compassion for humanity in me and I wanted to let people know that the discomfort could be dropped and The Guiding Principle could be known and enjoyed. I became extremely sensitive and could feel people's emotional energy field: it was seeing without eyes.

Again I had the feeling that this was actually our natural state of being which had simply been forgotten. I could see that this was always available to every single person and there was nothing special about what I perceived. In fact I understood that it was profoundly ordinary and had always been there, except the maelstrom of thoughts and agitation constantly overshadowed it.

Without so much of my vital capacity being used to maintain the belief in a virtual identity, there was suddenly an abundance of energy to nourish the other aspects of my being.

Life appeared to become very multi-dimensional and I perceived The Guiding Principle dancing through reality, connecting the invisible with the visible - bringing people together, flowing through words and actions, playing birdsong through birds.

LAUGHTER

Once or twice over the coming weeks I tried to help people who emitted a strong energy of unhappiness and quickly understood it wasn't that straightforward. One day when I was writing in a café, a young woman in her thirties came in and sat at the next table. I immediately felt that she had recently let go of a long-cherished dream, and without thinking I asked her why it wasn't possible to do what she loved most in life.

She almost fell off her chair and sobbed her heart out for nearly an hour. Through the sobs she explained that she had just abandoned her studies to become a Cranial Sacral healer because of financial problems. It took three cups of tea and a lot of reassurance to calm things down, before she finally left with a look of complete confusion on her face.

Other unexpected and often mysterious things started to happen.

I lost the habitual compulsion of constantly trying to put things right and fill in life's natural gaps with either words or actions. Everything started to sort itself out without me needing to know how or even why. My job it appeared was only to see the wonder – touch the wonder of life as it naturally expressed itself through me. Friends would call round eager for advice and all I could do was hand them a drum, even if they insisted that they couldn't drum. We always astonished ourselves with the amazing rhythms that transpired and they would leave feeling completely resolved. I also sensed that something had been resolved in me too.

A delightful by-product of that day face down in the mud, was the laugher and deeply healing humor that seemed to skip through life as a result of clearly seeing through the stories that my mind projected. I could actually enjoy them instead of stressing out. And seeing that God must have a brilliant sense of humor washed all the heaviness away. I know that doesn't make rational sense but there's no other way to describe it.

I remember meeting a friend for coffee in Hampstead, London to discuss a huge drama that was unfolding for him: it was very serious and he was extremely agitated.

I watched anger flash across his face as he began describing his situation. I was normally a very good listener. Years of coaching and guiding people had made me highly effective at unravelling stories and liberating solutions. However on this occasion I was surprised that despite a very clear description of events, I absolutely couldn't follow the thread of what he was saying. It sounded beautiful though – an abstract language made of light with no meaning: it all seemed beautifully lost.

It crossed my mind that we are all beautifully lost. And as my friend's angry words morphed and wove into this wonderful, sacred tongue, a huge inner smile rose up inside me, until I could no longer contain my joy at not having a clue what he was saying. I began laughing and it was such a wonderful feeling.

At this point, much to his astonishment, my friend also discovered that he couldn't follow the thread of his own story. As I shook with laughter he frantically searched for the correct order of events and some form of meaning, but to no avail: the story was vanishing like early morning mist.

At that point with fire in his eyes he accused me of pulling some kind of mind trick on him. But it had nothing to do with me.

Eventually, as his search floundered, and all the pieces that had once formed his drama scattered here and there, he too mysteriously found himself laughing.

Our combined laughter was so embodied and so cleansing that we both completely disappeared into it. At one point I couldn't even remember my name or who this other amazing being laughing back at me was. It felt truly blissful.

People sitting near us in the coffee shop couldn't help themselves and also began laughing. This was life setting itself free and it wasn't going to be contained.

My friend called me a few days later. He was now even more amused and confused, explaining how the other people embroiled in the drama had also mysteriously completely lost the thread of events and grievances. Apparently the whole thing had eventually collapsed into laughter with friendships restored and healed.

VISION

Another characteristic of this kind of perceptual and physical realignment, or return to the natural state, was a series of astonishingly blinding headaches. They would start with a feeling of something spiralling up from the base of my spine towards my head. At first I actually thought that something was crawling around inside my body and wondered if this was possible. In many ways it had the characteristics of rising Kundalini energy but unfortunately without the crescendo of bliss.

When the headaches were in full flow, large, painful swellings would erupt from my head like mini volcanoes, and from my perception appeared to belch out what I can only describe as a dark, cloudy energy. I was surprised that no one else could see it. My wife Esther could feel it though and would clam it down with her gentle, loving and healing touch.

On one occasion, these swellings became so severe that I blacked out with the pain and fell to the floor. I was out for just a few seconds, but on coming round, I saw the world in a kaleidoscope of phenomenally beautiful fractal patterns. It took my breath away. Not knowing quite what had happened, both Esther and I thought it wise to at least get this checked out at the hospital. And after several hours of doctors shining lights into my eyes and making concerned sounds, they eventually suggested a brain scan, but I was already heading for the door. By this time a deep knowing had arisen that it was nothing to be worried about.

I discovered that I could find my way around very easily and sat on Hampstead Heath enjoying my new vision. I was really quite happy to see the world this way, and the more I settled into it the more I was able to pick things out that were obscured by the mechanism of normal sight. Like the dot paintings which reveal a hidden three-dimensional image when observed in a particular way, new visions were unveiled.

I saw what looked like spirits emerging from trees and great waves of energetic colour sweeping through people as they walked past. When I tried explaining this later, many friends suggested that it sounded like an LSD trip. Except this was completely different to any drug experience – it wasn't a different reality; life was naturally and spontaneously pouring out of emptiness. Moreover, it didn't feel particularly strange; rather it felt more natural than my ordinary way of seeing.

The fractal vision lasted the best part of a week before disappearing as quickly and mysteriously as it had arrived.

With the passing of each headache I would feel a tremendous lightness and freedom, as if I'd been cleansed of something heavy. On one occasion I was travelling on the London Underground when a terrible headache flooded into my head. Staggering off the train I found a platform bench just as my entire mind seemed to burst open into a space of complete euphoria. The utter beauty flooding forth from even the most mundane object was so powerful that all I could do was sit and watch in astonishment. I must have remained on the bench for nearly two hours before the torrent of beauty finally began to subside, and I could make my way out of the station. On reflection the dingy, litter-strewn station of Elephant & Castle was an unlikely place to be overwhelmed with beauty, and yet there it was ever-present in the dirt and dust.

During this phase I developed a strong dislike for coffee and alcohol. Already being a vegetarian, I now found that my body wanted less and less cooked food and any desire for sugar and dairy completely vanished.

All spiritual practices ground to a halt and I lost any desire to take the amazing shamanic medicine, Ayahuasca and participate in the sacred rituals. This had become a great teacher and healer. It had given me many beautiful insights and experiences and yet it now seemed as if there was no longer anything to seek or to find in practices, rituals or medicines. The only things that I still felt drawn to do were drumming, singing, chanting and a movement practice that I had learnt many years ago and almost forgotten.

Over the following months I became increasingly familiar with The Guiding Principle and how it shapes our lives. The experience of my mind apparently harmonising with The Guiding Principle appeared to take place as a result of becoming aware of its existence: and finally surrendering to it. Without this awareness life appeared to need our intervention and control. In my own mind I noticed the distinctive quality of thoughts that were in harmony with The Guiding Principle and those that were not aligned. The thoughts in harmony had a distinctive resonance. They appeared to come alive in my mind, whereas other thoughts appeared far less vital. A mind pulsing with thoughts in harmony with The Guiding Principle literally comes alive; illuminated from within its own unique patterns as they arise.

I noticed how creativity in all forms had the effect of harmonising us with the Guiding Principle. Of course I had heard such things many times and felt this myself, yet I had never truly perceived it so intimately and fully. But at the same, and paradoxically in many ways, I saw that creativity didn't direct The Guiding principle in any way. Our viewpoint of creativity could change and yet The Guiding Principle was always complete, therefore creativity was a projector of it or a delivery system for it. I will be explaining this in greater depth later on.

EFFORTLESS

These insights and experiments would eventually form the basis of The Guiding Principle *openings* and *pointers* covered in this text. But at that stage I had no idea that this could be shared in any practical way.

Once I had directly perceived The Guiding Principle I saw how hard and unforgiving my life had previously been without touching this wonder. It doesn't have to be, but for the most part, we tend to run around trying to control things that are ultimately beyond our capacity to understand or influence. This causes incredible tension in both our bodies and minds.

It was effortless to simply let The Guiding Principle move me. It seemed totally obvious that even a simple thought is in fact a cosmic event, not an isolated happening. I instinctively understood that the will I had always assumed to be my own, was in fact the same will that moved the wind through the trees and the same will that directed light photons towards the Earth from the Sun. What I had taken to be something that I alone had ownership of and dominion over was always moved by The Guiding Principle. I had never been in control nor could I ever be in control of anything. The distinction was amazingly subtle, totally obvious when seen, but nevertheless revelatory. Far from everything descending into anarchy as this might suggest, I saw that the world and what appeared as my life effortlessly falls into place. And for the first time since being a tiny child, life took on an unburdened and spontaneous quality.

The net result physically, was a dropping away of huge amounts of tension apparently held in my body. I unexpectedly found that I was far suppler and the nagging aches and pains in my neck and shoulders, which had become almost permanent fixtures, completely vanished. I would walk around delighting in the miraculous fact that I was alive and able to move. It felt like the first time – independent of drugs or shamanic medicines - that I'd really and truly noticed what it was like to be alive in a human body – to feel blood coursing through arteries and the breeze brushing against my face. It felt as if everything was engaged in the most sacred and intimate conversation.

I increasingly saw that everyone contains the possibility to know The Guiding Principle and experience the relaxed knowing of where life desires us to go. The Guiding Principle has no desire or will but appears as if this were the case. The *experience* of intensely desiring something is The Guiding Principle and yet it contains absolutely no desire. It creates anything out of nothing.

The balance between seeing and not seeing is so delicate. Our paths through life are entwined in illusions that prevent our true nature from shining through.

I understood that when our experience of life is transformed, everything else is transformed: it's a non-local event - meaning all of life moves towards greater harmony with The Guiding Principle, all of life moves towards a recognition of its own miracle.

And yet even bestowed with so many insights and realisations, as time moved on, life with all its twists and turns periodically seemed to conceal a clear seeing of The Guiding Principle. Thankfully the sorrow, fear and turmoil never returned but the tangible sense of what I had come to experience as The Guiding Principle drifted into the distance, more like a half-remembered dream. My mind would fish around in reality looking for it, desiring to touch its brilliance once again.

The flow of life, the good and the challenging continued. I found tremendous enjoyment in some things and frustration in other things. I understood that the dances our actions create and the stories we weave, are nothing more than beautiful patterns. I took to really looking at these patterns and seeing their unique beauty. In essence the following months turned out to be a time of integration and reflection.

I started to incorporate what I had discovered and what I saw into my life coaching and the talks I gave. I was amazed at how people were able to joyfully let go of deeply entrenched issues as a result of me sharing simple discoveries. I was present for people in a different way because there was no longer anything in me trying to get something from them or change them: I simply accepted them and held the space for their hearts to open and their aliveness to be fully felt.

People would ask me, how do we let go of the old, painful version of ourselves? And I would hear myself answering:

"Once you have accepted who you have become as a result of following what wasn't true, your transformation will be activated. Your time has come and your own unique truth will begin to move you: this is how we all start."

As soft and light as a new borne fowl wobbling on its stick legs, we arrive at the real dance of life. We stop shuffling around on the edge and move to the centre of our life.

It was obvious that The Guiding Principle was at work even if I had lost sight of it.

LIFE MOVING LIFE

It would be a several months before I once again directly experienced The Guiding Principle. It began with Esther giving me a powerful hypnotherapy session, to gain clarity around actions I needed to take to move forward with a project. During the session I unearthed a very old pattern which in the past had held me back from fully expressing myself. I had considered it fully resolved, dug out from the root. So I was really surprised to see it arrogantly sitting there, as if I'd never done a single bit of work to clear it.

Over the previous few months I had begun to regularly attend meetings in Highgate, London with a Non-Duality teacher called, Roger Linden. Non-Duality is an experience in which there is no separation between subject and object: a "me" and the rest of the universe, a "me" and Nature. Our inner and outer realities are one and the same.

From a place of great clarity, Roger speaks about letting go of the strains and stresses of maintaining an identity that doesn't actually exist. Out of many people I'd heard speak on this subject, I found Roger's talks particularly direct and powerful.

I had booked to go to one of his meetings just after my hypnotherapy session with Esther. I decided to take the annoying belief pattern that had just resurfaced along too, and let it stew in an atmosphere of clear seeing.

During the meeting I felt uncharacteristically aggravated. Nevertheless I sat and listened to what Roger had to say. I left the meeting with the same aggravation still simmering away beneath the surface. And as I went to open the door of my car a great crack echoed up from the base of my spine and at the same time a glacier stillness embraced everything including me. There was no thought and no time passing and, like before, there was awareness despite the absence of time and thought. And in that stillness, the dynamic Intelligence that I called The Guiding Principle swept through and reanimated it all: it brought everything to life.

It reanimated and vitalised what appeared to be me and it reanimated and vitalised what appeared as the world. But there was simply a complete knowing that nothing was separate from it, and everything that it brought to life through its own mysterious power source was an expression of that same Intelligence.

At the point where time appeared to re-launch itself, the remaining thread attaching me to a belief in separation, stretched and finally broke. And once again there was just complete ease and acceptance of life exactly as it was. There was no desire for anything to be different because there was just a resonance of fullness.

There was a sense that Roger Linden's words had somehow worked away at loosening that final thread.

Similar to the time after I buried myself in the earth, thoughts and feelings continued rising and falling but there was no ownership of them. In that freedom, what appeared as me, moved to get into the car. But it was The Guiding Principle that directed this experience and every infinitesimal detail of the experience: life moving life: Nature experiencing its own dynamic nature.

I understood that this is what is always taking place and even the *not seeing* or *not knowing* of this is yet another experience animated by The Guiding Principle. And finally it was seen that although the pure, thoughtless space at first appeared to be what The Guiding Principle operated in, they were in fact one and the same. Even the impression that one existed inside the other was merely an appearance. Somehow in the mystery there was stillness and there was dynamic or vitalised stillness. This was utterly fascinating and amazing!

I drove home and Esther and I played some musical instruments together before going to bed. Everything simply carried on.

But through the grace of The Guiding Principle, pure Consciousness had become the ultra-alive sensory organ through which life was directly experienced. This expanded viewpoint replaced what had previously been seen as a separate me, experiencing life through the filter of the five senses. The normally perceived senses of touch, sight, smell, hearing and taste were still fully present, except they were now phenomena arising in a vaster spectrum of reality. In essence they no longer served a belief in separation.

Consequently it became obvious that there is no limit to what can be experienced and thus the possibilities are infinite.

Paradoxically though, there was a real enjoyment of all my unique characteristics and experiences. I felt more alive and more engaged with life as a result of no longer referencing my identity exclusively from thoughts or mind. Feeling the intimate touch of The Guiding Principle, knowing that it breathed vitality into everything, had the effect of igniting a deep fascination with the detail of life, all the intricate connections that appeared to manifest as events happening.

Again, paradoxically and somewhat mysteriously, although the belief, or perhaps more accurately, the habit of 'me' had dissolved, I felt more like me than I'd ever felt. I had no idea how this could be, but at the same time I wasn't complaining. I carried on doing 'Davide' kind of things in the same way that a particular tree or animal expresses its own individual qualities, unfolding through unique patterns. All of these qualities and patterns were effortlessly delivered into the flow of experience. To see this so clearly was incredible.

The difference between this opening to The Guiding Principle and the previous seeing, was that it was known that nothing could in reality diminish or come and go. I felt that every possible question was being answered in each moment of existence: the answers were contained in whatever experience was arising.

Having more or less abandoned all my shamanic practices, along with yoga and meditation, over the next couple of weeks, I felt my enthusiasm reignite. I resumed them: a pattern spontaneously unfolding in its own way. I also began reshaping my talks and introducing different ideas into discussions. Creative and playful ways to help people disengage from stress and struggle became increasingly obvious and I offered these methods up for people to play and experiment with. I can't say that these were 'teachings', rather they were offered as *openings* and *pointers*. I saw that nothing could be predicted and each and every one of us arrives at the truth in a unique way. My *openings* and *pointers* merely serve the purpose of gently reminding us of the miracle we all share. At our deepest level this is always known.

AMAZING QUALITY OF EXPERIENCE

Following that day I left Roger Linden's meeting to simply get into my car, The Guiding Principle has been vibrantly alive in my perception. Importantly, it's not a special state because it is always present and always will be, regardless of whether or not it's consciously perceived. So when I take people through the process of dissolving the patterns of thought that are simply directing them away from seeing, they realise that they have never been separate from God and never can be separate. Life can then flow along without concepts preventing that seeing.

This doesn't mean that they may not once again lose sight, as I did. But they have stepped out of the realm of limitation once, so the possibility is there, always present. The openness to enquire is available and this material provides a framework for that enquiry.

After that final opening to The Guiding Principle, events moved quickly. I often joked that if Davide were doing this, it probably wouldn't work. I began sharing some of the things I had discovered with people who were searching for answers to their discomfort with life. And they started to experience a sense of freedom from perceived limitations and discover a greater sense of joy in their lives. It then seemed very natural to offer these ways of exploring and playing with life to a wider audience. The result of this desire to share what I have been shown is what you are about to investigate for yourself.

My creative repertoire is constantly evolving as The Guiding Principle leads me to play with greater abandon and energy. These ideas may well grow and transform in their own time. In a sense this may be just the beginning: we'll see what happens.

I have no great concern with ideas of spirituality, enlightenment or anything similar. For me such things represent abstract concepts and carry meanings that don't really match with what I'm talking about in this exploration. This is not about reaching some mystical state.

It's about living naturally, free of tension and absolutely free of the past. It's about living in wonder of what possibilities will be delivered by the grace of Nature.

People ask me if The Guiding Principle is the same as Chi energy, and the answer is that all phenomena – including Chi energy - are brought to life by The Guiding Principle. This vast intelligence possesses no energy or characteristics of its own that can be channeled or harnessed. Chi energy, spiritual experiences, the sun on your face, drinking a glass of water are all delivered into the realm of experience: ultimately there is no difference between them.

You may notice I will use words such as, God, The Mind of God, Presence, The Divine, Unity, Spaciousness and Nature with a capital 'N'. These words are an attempt to communicate what everything, including The Guiding Principle, appears to arise in. I'm a speaker and these words please me, and seem to carry a power or resonance that most of us easily recognise. They point to something that exists beyond concepts.

In addition, even though The Guiding Principle is the dynamic aspect of Presence and ultimately they are one and the same, The Guiding Principle still appears to arise within Presence. This is only an appearance but I make this distinction for the benefit of communicating ideas and observations.

What I'm ultimately passionate about is opening you to the possibility of having an amazing quality of experience in your life. I have no way of knowing whether the ideas and methods I share with you will facilitate or lead you to a similar experience of life as mine.
I have no ability to inspect anyone's consciousness to find such a thing out. I keep an open mind and consider the possibility that there are beings – maybe even human beings – that possess such

abilities and knowledge. But in the absence of these powers, all I have to go on is what people have told me after using The Guiding Principle material.

The possibility to experience and know The Guiding Principle exists in everyone, always. And ultimately there is nothing real preventing that knowing. This is not about special techniques, powers or tricks of the mind. It is not about acquiring or adding anything. The best way for me to describe what you are about to explore is the **'stopping of not seeing'** and the practice of **'knowing instead of not knowing'**.

To be at ease with life is your birthright and I suggest that this simple fact is the barometer for your journey through this material.

My job in all this is to simply practice what I do, share my discoveries and offer them up with passion, creativity and laughter. I possess nothing special and contain no more truth than you. We equally share a connection to the miracle of life. This book is a sharing rather than a teaching.

I don't pretend to understand The Guiding Principle and yet we can know it as our own nature and bask in its glory. We can feel its touch as we move through the world of thoughts and things.

Beyond any words, the most powerful thing is to directly experience The Guiding Principle for yourself, and I leave it up to you to create your own unique descriptions. As I've just said, this is about the *stopping of not seeing* and facilitating an environment where fixed ideas can be released. There is no end product or certificate to say you've arrived or qualified, so there's nothing to achieve in any conventional sense.

There's a saying: 'sometimes we have to use a thorn to remove a thorn'. So some of what we will be exploring together will be the presentation of a concept to remove a concept. If you feel yourself fighting against anything just sit with it, there's no need to prove anything one way or the other. Any concepts I present will work away on their own, no need to force anything......

Connecting with The Guiding Principle will show you things that you cannot yet imagine. It's possible to discover just how natural it is to be joyful and feel fully alive. Whatever happens, you will discover more about who you are and become increasingly open to the possibility of life being lived as a miracle.

Opening ~ One

THOUGHTS DO NOT CAUSE ACTIONS

This is perhaps one of the most difficult and even unsettling considerations for many people. My aim is not to unsettle you but to free you from what is creating disharmony and detrimental to your life experience. With everything that I offer, the only test is always your own experience: there is only your experience of reality.

The belief that our thoughts lead to actions is so engrained in our human psyche that it can seem impossible for it not to be so. We have so much invested in this belief - so much of our history, ethics, philosophy and values. It underpins the very structure and workings of our culture.

On the surface, the possibility that thoughts are *not* the cause of our actions seems to deprive us of cherished qualities such as free will and choice; what is generally called self-determination.

It's almost universally believed that we are self-determined beings. However, by exploring our direct experience of life with a willingness to go beyond what we've been told is true, we become receptive to something far more astonishing.

From my current experience of life it is clear that a fixed belief *that thoughts cause actions* - a fixed belief that our thoughts are the determining factor - reinforces a tension that sustains the feeling of separation: this tension is an ever subtle resistance to The Guiding Principle.

The teacher Roger Linden very accurately describes how the belief in separation causes a series of *"subtle but very powerful contractions in the body"*. He goes on to describe how these contractions reinforce the misconception that there is a person inside the head and body experiencing life and choreographing actions.

When this subtle resistance, contraction or particular pattern in the mind is no longer present, a shift naturally takes place.

In essence instead of being self-determined, what appears as *you*, becomes SELF-determined or God-determined. Instead of a separate entity set adrift in a vast world of uncertainty, confusion and often fear, the possibility exists for our minds to become harmonised with The Guiding Principle, the Mind of God. And when this harmonising takes place the turbulence that characterises so much of our thoughts settles down. The mind begins to see its own limitations and stops struggling to maintain a false sense of control: this is a truly beautiful process.

It is seen that instead of a loss of choice we become immersed in and embraced by the spontaneous flow of Nature. This is such a joyful and miraculous way of seeing compared to the tension of a separate 'self' feeling that it is alone and responsible for shifting atoms and controlling reality. Far from becoming detached, we actually become more intimately involved in the process of life. Consciousness becomes aware of itself in a body and a mind. What appears as 'our life' then takes on the quality of being in service of the Divine. This appearance of being in service of the Divine can arise as a feeling of empowerment and a dropping away of the compulsion to constantly try and control life.

People ask me if the shift to living from The Guiding Principle means that we stop creating dreams and taking actions to manifest them. And the simple answer is 'No'. It doesn't mean that we no longer take action to create things, plan or set goals. We still employ the faculty of logic and make judgments: all of those things continue to take place. However movements in the mind are no longer seen as personal, and yet at the same time there is this incredible intimacy with life that goes way beyond how reality was previously experienced. In this intimacy with life it becomes clear which dreams contain power and are free of tension and unnecessary drama, and there is a natural movement towards them. So in this sense the constant drive to figure life out can either greatly diminish or completely vanish.

We are all familiar with what athletes, musicians, inventors, scientists and artists refer to as 'the Zone', and most of us have had direct experience of this. People frequently describe the Zone as feeling as if time has stopped or slowed down and their actions are guided by a greater power. In the absence of thoughts, there's a sense of connectedness, ease or wellbeing, and a knowing of what to do. This is The Guiding Principle moving life.

This Zone is perceived when our sense of separation and thoughts fall away and we become one with what's arising in the moment. We are shown that there is only the one vast intelligence at work.

It's possible to see that there is no separate cause for anything happening in the manifest world - the movement of all life arises from The Guiding Principle, which has no form and no energy. In the same way that a scientist may know that a particle has a negative or a positive charge but nothing to say about how that charge came to be there, The Guiding Principle also appears to be an enigma. That is, until it is 'realised'. Once it's seen that we are already what we're looking for, there is nothing more to seek. Suddenly everything we will ever need to know about existence is present in our direct experience.

However, when our identity is referenced purely from the mind we don't recognize The Guiding Principle – we don't recognize ourselves as God. The mind appears to have dominion and we face the turbulence of being immersed in the patterns of thoughts. There is the constant bafflement at why we appear to think one thing and do something completely different.

Anxiety and tension arise through feeling at odds with our true nature. When our identity is not referenced purely from the mind, thoughts appear in much the same way as weather patterns, with their own slipstreams and characteristics. I have a strong knowing that these patterns are not random or chaotic: I don't believe the concept of random has ever been proved. The constant movement of thoughts seems to play an integral part in the greater picture of reality. I sometimes see them as part of an energetic stream turning an unimaginably vast, ethereal turbine that powers Universal Wisdom. Ultimately everything is a pattern of light unfolding, weaving elegant symmetries and order into the Universe.

When it is seen that thoughts do not cause actions a huge amount of energy is withdrawn from the mind. There's suddenly an innocence and freshness to thoughts when they no longer support the illusion of separation. It becomes obvious that no separate entity has the power to bring thoughts into existence.

However, until this is realised, the suggestion that we are not responsible for our thoughts can spark a great deal of controversy. It can seem like an attempt to abandon responsibility. We will explore responsibility later, but for now the seeing that thoughts are not something that we have ownership of or dominion over doesn't for one minute mean that what appears as responsibility or morality stops happening. In fact it's seen that life is always moving to take care of itself. This movement is hidden through believing in the potency of thoughts to instigate actions.

The mind always follows The Guiding Principle and in reality never brings anything into being.

So what we call the mind is an immense non-physical mechanism swirling with thoughts. The mind perceives the directive of The Guiding Principle, and seeing the instigation of actions it almost immediately claims ownership. But what's really happening is more like the mind trying to follow a wonderful and elaborate dance without knowing the steps. The mind has become so adept at this improvisation that actions and thoughts appear to happen simultaneously. Mind always moves to synchronise itself with The Guiding Principle, and the illusion of it being the creator of actions is established. The mind keeps up the dance, constantly following The Guiding Principle's lead.

It is an expert at filling in the gaps to create the appearance of continuity and synchronisation. So when I talk of the mind falling into the service of The Guiding Principle, what seems to happen is the pretence of it being the creator of actions drops away. The mind then becomes available to serve life in a different way.

Much laughter arises in the discussions and interactions I have with people these days, as I offer a natural way to unravel the often tangled webs we weave around situations. People come to me frustrated at what appear to be the same old patterns repeating again and again. On the surface, the struggle to free oneself of the pattern creates an even bigger and tighter tangle. That is until it is known that believing in the validity of those patterns is seeing something that was never there in the first place - creating the false impression of being trapped.

When we stop struggling, the web that appears to bind us loosens and eventually falls away. This often creates great swathes of laughter – it's really beautiful. We feel what it's like to be free of a restriction. Importantly though, everything is realised at the right time: not an instant before. Therefore there is never anything wrong or out of place with where you are. Everything is in prefect balance.

One kind of question that I get asked when I talk of thoughts not causing actions is:

"How come people appear to transform their circumstances when there is a change in the way they think? They may attend a course or receive new information and start to think differently about a situation. And as a result take very different actions. Surely this is proof that thoughts do in fact cause actions?"

On the surface this may well appear to be what is happening. And yet if we journey deeper there is only ever The Guiding Principle dancing life into being. Prior to any thought there was pure potential or Consciousness without form. Out of pure potential there arose an impulse to change. This was never created by thoughts and it was never the personal directive of a separate being, existing in isolation from Nature.

If thoughts actually caused actions we would not survive for long without going completely insane. Imagine trying to do even the simplest thing solely at the bidding of thoughts arising in your mind.

Judging by the incessant and uncontrollable stream of thoughts that arises in our minds, even making a cup of tea would lead to a complete breakdown.

The possibility of transformation arises spontaneously in, or more accurately, out of the Mind of God; and is shaped by The Guiding Principle, the dynamic aspect of stillness. Both the possibility of transformation and the actual transformation itself are The Guiding Principle. There is no separate entity which has to control the infinite variables needed to create that transformation.

Beneath the surface appearance of a separate individual all the variables have already been taken care of, and the environment created in which the transformation can appear to take place. The great dance of life is happening prior to even a single thought. Thoughts then fall into step with the dance and appear to be the instigators of a desire to take a course, see a teacher or gather new information. There is no separate personal doer involved, only the illusion of a separate doer now having different thoughts and experiencing change as a result. Everything was always totally taken care of. And what appears as our separate life is always totally taken care of in every moment. This is the miracle living us right now – we are only this.

When our identity is no longer referenced from thoughts, it is seen that our actions are an aspect of Nature's patterns. In this same way, the characteristics that appear as you or me, are seen as beautiful patterns in Nature. These patterns fit perfectly into the patterns of all other manifestations: the ebb and flow of energy, of humans, animals, the elements, the planet, the solar system and on and on.

The absence of feeling separate from the very thing that orchestrates life gives rise to a simple wonder in whatever arises. This shift in viewpoint takes the sting out of life and rubs healing balm on our fear and discomfort. This mystery which is far greater than anything we can imagine, facilitates life lived from a new perspective. A perspective that's unrecognisable from what was previously believed to be who and what we are.

As I have said, when The Guiding Principle recognises its own radiance being expressed through what appears as your life, there is a falling away of the constant seeking to resolve a disconnection or loss that never in fact happened. And because that loss never took place, The Guiding Principle is all that's happening now. This is what can be realised in an instant without any further discussion or consideration.

All I can do is open you to the possibility of your own unique realisation and use pointers to help potentialise that possibility – making that possibility potent. There are many pointers residing in the story that I've just told of how I came to recognise The Guiding Principle. You will naturally take away what you need from that story. You don't need to apply effort and force to reap the benefits of this sharing. Get a feel for where each word is pointing, rather than trying to grasp what is being said intellectually.

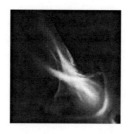

Pointer ~ 1

SOFTEN TO LIFE

To maintain tension requires an enormous amount of vital energy. We learn to contract away and protect ourselves from what we perceive as *the threat of life*. Mostly we feel that there's a separate entity inside our head which somehow needs to hold all of reality together. The strain created by this feeling constantly strengthens the illusion of separation, leading to energy restrictions in the physical body or a self-contraction. The combination of mental and physical contractions create a general background static of tension and anxiety, preventing us from openly embracing and being embraced by life. The greater the contraction the more separate we feel, leading to a self-perpetuating mechanism for separation.

Remember I spoke about becoming SELF- determined instead of self-determined. And the process of softening to life creates a spaciousness in which the mismatches between actions and thoughts become apparent. In a space created by softening to life The Guiding Principle can become revealed: the true SELF is revealed.

So in softening to life we soften our white-knuckled grip on the world, our compulsion to try and control everyone and everything. This involves softening your breath and softening your belly: a gentle letting go of tension held in your muscles. There's no need to sit or try to meditate, this softening can be done regardless of what you are doing. It begins by simply noticing where there is tension and tightness in your belly and in your breath and accepting that there is tension. Just accept the tension. This is all that's required, no need to try and relax. This noticing naturally and effortlessly begins to free your innate wisdom from the shackles of tension. Your body already knows how to relax in the same way that a fledgling already knows how to fly.

I remember feeling that if I let go of my grip on life for even a second everything would come crashing down. And yet surprisingly when everything is let go of, life continues to unfold far more beautifully than before. It was seen that my tight grip on reality served absolutely no purpose other than holding together an uncomfortable illusion.

Relaxing the breath automatically quietens agitation in the mind, and you will notice that it's difficult to jump back into a stressful past or conjure up a stressful future without tensing the breath and belly. The breath is so simple and so direct; it lets us know exactly what's going on. There's no need to practice because you are guided: your breath is already a master of meditation, automatically feeding you the elixir of life. Your breath is The Guiding Principle revealed in each and every moment.

There's actually no need to hold on to life because it can't go anywhere without taking you with it. Even when the last breath has left our lips The Guiding Principle continues to deliver us straight into the open arms of Unconditional Love. That is its nature - all it can ever do: it is utterly relentless. Nothing, not even what we believe to be death, can stop it delivering us into the open arms of God.

Next, begin to literally soften your focus on the external world and also allow your inner sight or mind's eye to soften too. Relax the strain of trying to reach out into the world or journeying into your mind, searching for images. Begin to notice that the experience of shapes, colours and movement is being effortlessly delivered. An inner illumination effortlessly shines upon the images spontaneously arising in your mind.

As this softening settles, notice that there is a Presence – something that doesn't come and go – which effortlessly accommodates the knowing of both these different ways of seeing. In both cases the experience of seeing is being painted onto the clear canvas of this Presence. Seeing is directly registered and known in Presence, it isn't us seeing.

The incredibly complex connections and mysterious synchronicities that comprise the experiences of seeing, hearing and feeling are woven together and delivered, without you needing to know any of the mechanics. You don't need to know how to translate the language of light photons, or how to move sound through the air. This is all completely taken care of. Whatever you are seeing, hearing and feeling is taken care of.

This is the nature of everything you experience. Everything is effortlessly registered in a totally stable and totally accepting Presence. So it can become apparent that you don't have *to do* anything to know that something is being experienced. If you reach out and touch ice you don't have to create the experience of cold: it's totally taken care of. This is life unfolding naturally.

All thoughts are delivered into the same totally stable and accepting Presence without you needing to create the unimaginable physics of thoughts. The experience of thinking is automatically registered in the never-changing Presence. When this is noticed, it's possible to also notice the effortless quality of those thoughts arising and falling away. What's noticing is Presence itself. You are not thinking thoughts into being, they are 'given' life – life is unconditionally given to them as it is to everything else.

The power that delivers reality in the form of experience is simply the most abundant thing possible; all it does is give unconditionally.

This is the characteristic of The Guiding Principle embracing us and taking care of everything always.

It's possible to bring this same softening to your physical actions. Notice how the experience of moving – even a tiny movement – once again is effortlessly registered in the never-changing Presence that accepts everything. This is the case regardless of whether the movement is pleasurable or painful – the experience is automatically 'brought to life' in Presence. This is The Guiding Principle bringing pure potentiality to life, sculpting nothing into something.

That day I lay facedown in the mud, my entire body racked with pain, I discovered that even pain, both mental and physical, is always falling back into the embrace of God. Softening to pain is the bridge across the river of suffering.

Everything is resolved in the instant it is experienced, all sorrow and all despair are only ever falling back into that one Presence which is nothing other than God, and nothing other than who you are beyond the constructs of the mind. All actions are falling back into God and all thoughts are falling back into God. This fact can be realised in this very moment: you are effortlessly falling into God and The Guiding Principle is effortlessly delivering you back and birthing new experiences. Everything is inseparable from nothing; fullness is inseparable from emptiness.

Softening to life extends to loosening your grip on rigid patterns that cause you to contract and forget that you are falling back into God. This includes rigid patterns in your relationships, in your work and in your health. Soften your words and let them fall back into silence, the Mind of God. And as you do this, the silence between your words becomes a conversation with The Guiding Principle as it delivers the next word you will speak. Will it be a word in the service of the Divine or a word to perpetuate forgetting? Notice which, before it falls back into God.

There is a prayer I say before I begin writing, giving a talk, a workshop or an interview:

"Be soft, let my words match your words so together we speak the source of life back into the world."

Soften, soften and soften to this utter abundance and the never-ending acceptance of everything that is given.

Soften your grip on things that you instinctively know you don't need. Instead allow life to lavish you with the abundance of experience: this is not an ideology - it's ALIVENESS!

In the recognition that life is living itself effortlessly and naturally, the present moment can be nothing other than perfect.

Opening ~ Two

EVERYTHING IS SHOWING US THE TRUTH

Nothing is Hidden

I was thirty-nine when my mother died. On the five consecutive nights after her death, I experienced being totally lucid whilst dreaming. I would journey across a timeless realm to meet her in a hypnotically beautiful building or location. One in particular was a spectacular butterfly house where each sumptuously patterned butterfly seemed to contain the spirit of one of my mother's past lives: it was absolutely extraordinary!

In each dream we would walk and have a conversation about what it was like to be dead. She appeared to be quite elated with death. She was young and strong, surrounded by a soft, silvery aura. She appeared younger than me and free of time. It seemed that death was everything that she could possibly have wished for in life and infinitely more.

I remember asking her why she was so happy to be dead. She threw back her head laughing.

"There is nothing to hold onto any more, and there is so much freedom in seeing this", she replied.

I remember finding her answer amusing and wondered if the same could be true for the living.

Present and fully lucid in these dreams, I had the most joyful feeling that everything I encountered, including myself, contained the essence of some miraculous truth. And upon waking I would momentarily forget that I was no longer in the dream and still experience this feeling as my eyes focused on objects in the bedroom. Then remembering that I was no longer dreaming, a thought arose that I could lose the ability to sense this, and it would instantly vanish.

On the fifth night I explained what was happening to my mother. We were sitting in a magical garden filled with fragrant, fecund flowers. She looked concerned, and reaching into her extravagant 1950's handbag, withdrew a gold fountain pen and a piece of ivory writing paper. Resting the paper on the side of the handbag, she busied herself writing and after a few seconds handed me the paper. "There we are," she said, "This should help."

I read what she had written in her lovely italicised handwriting. It made complete sense to me. The dream carried on and we talked a bit more until she announced that this was the last time we would meet. There was not the slightest hint of sadness or attachment in her voice, and perhaps because of this, I also didn't feel any sadness: in fact I felt delighted.

However after the dream I struggled to remember what she had written on the paper. I felt annoyed that I hadn't given it more attention. I then proceeded to spend days trying to trace back through the dream, but to no avail. As time passed any sense of what the words might have been was swept away in the constant stream of life.

I had more or less completely forgotten this missing element of the dream until the evening I left Roger Linden's meeting. Driving home I became fully aware of what my mother had written in the dream, and after so many years I felt both surprised and happy at the same time.

Her words were:

"Every experience is truth. This is life realising itself in every imaginable form. Everything is vitally alive with the truth, be it extraordinary or mundane."

I have no idea how these two events appeared to join up, yet what had become completely apparent on that evening was this very truth.

It was also totally obvious that we all directly know – beyond intellect - that everything we encounter, including what we take to be our separate selves, tells the story of its Divine nature. This is absolutely known at our deepest level. It's as if God is speaking to us through every single thing we experience. But most of the time this communication is more like a faint message beamed from a distant galaxy. It becomes distorted and confused as it journeys through the turbulent atmosphere of thoughts. We end up believing that we are different from what appears as the world.

I also realised that there is nothing stored in any manifestation: everything is totally empty. So the truth of our Divine nature is not stored in objects, people, experiences or states: instead these 'objects', flowing from pure presence - deliver the truth: they are messengers.

This absolute seeing that everything is totally 'empty' has a very powerful affect on how life is experienced. No thoughts or behaviors are stored or contained inside us. We are wiped clean in every instant. What is believed to be a separate self is another set of experiences arising in Presence, delivering the Divine message into the manifest realm. The individual characteristics we appear to possess turn out to be unique ways in which the truth is expressed, regardless of whether or not we can see it.

What we call 'memories', are not thoughts, sounds or sensations stored in the brain, the mind or the body. The pulses of pure energy that constantly remake our bodies and the invisible dynamics of our minds are like the alphabet which forms the language of experiences. Importantly, the words, sentences and meanings of a language are not to be found in the alphabet because they exist only as a potential. Also much like the language of music, there are infinite variations that can be created from the simple base components.

Therefore what we believe to be memories relating to us, as separate individuals, are actually potentials spontaneously forming into unique experiences. These experiences never reside inside us, and neither can we have an identical memory experience twice: this is an illusion. Importantly, when this illusion is exposed we discover tremendous freedom and joy.

In the same way, when someone says that they keep having the same thought or memory, this can never be so. The mind is creating an illusion of continuity and we have the belief that this same thought is following us through time. Of course if it appears to be an inspiring thought why interfere with it? However, to see that disempowering and painful thoughts have no longevity or continuity is liberating to say the least.

Let's explore what is actually happening. Someone may have the belief that they keep thinking, 'I'm unsuccessful' and in turn believe this is directly causing them to be unsuccessful.

Now to create the thought pattern that gives rise to the experience of 'I'm unsuccessful', an almost unimaginable set of interlacing patterns and temporary relationships will be expressed through the mind/body system. It also includes the diverse array of influential factors in our physical environment. It begins with the invisible movement of pure energy, then the translating of this directive into electrical stimulation, firing neurons in the brain. The intricate mix of chemicals feeding the environment in which this activity is sustained includes oxygen and nutrients in the flowing blood supply. None of these things exist as fixed entities or realities in the mind or the body.

These patterns of neurons firing, liquids flowing, cellular activity, seem to be able to create auditory representations in the mind such as a critical voice of a parent or teacher. These may be accompanied by a host of dream-like visuals that appear to depict past failures, followed by sensations such as tightness in the solar plexus or head. All of these complex and intricate events are needed for this one thought process to arise, be perceived and finally fall away. Just realising the utter immensity of such a common occurrence can alone connect us to the miracle of life.

It's also important not to forget the falling away of a thought because this is all part of the process. Without it falling back into empty space and another thought arising, we would possess no ability to define it or know it was even present.

So when we begin to investigate and question our experience, the impossibility of this unique unfolding ever happening twice – let alone thousands of times - becomes apparent. Just as the same cloud can never appear twice in the sky, the same thought or group of thoughts can never be repeated. In just a matter of seconds the entire environment of mind, body and external factors has transformed.

The simple act of closing your eyes changes everything. I remember reading, and I've no idea how anyone can work this out, that one in-breath introduces a molecule from every single human being that has ever lived. So if we play with this, what happened to the separate 'you' that the previous thought appeared to happen in?

The same thoughts are never following you through time. So when it is known that these totally unique unfoldings have no continuity; it's also known that they possess no power to create failure in an imaginary future. There is no failure waiting to emerge from the shadows, there's only The Guiding Principle - infinite intelligence, weaving life together as fresh experiences.

And because of the direct availability of this seeing for everyone, there is always a space to recognize freedom. In seeing that no thought has a thread attached to some future unhappiness, what are you 'being moved' to create in this moment and the next moment? This is all that's ever happening: life is an open question with no need of an answer.

Crucially what I'm introducing is not science. I'm not a scientist and have only a very rudimentary understanding of science. I don't know how my computer works, and I have no idea what something like quantum physics actually is beyond supposedly dealing with tiny units of energy and strange things happening with light: it could be a fairy tale for all the difference it makes to my direct experience of life.

What I'm offering here can be verified or rejected by purely observing your own experience. Your freedom is directly available through your own experience – the qualitative aspect of reality - and you don't need any additional knowledge or extended wisdom to see this.

Your own experience of life can expose the misconception of a continuous life journeying through time. Seeing that what you took to be the same things repeating, are in fact unique arisings without any provable continuity can instantly break the *spell* of linear time.

Our minds create the illusion of time, of cause and effect, and therefore continuity. But in a far more miraculous way we are reborn in every moment. The only thing that has absolute continuity is the unchanging Presence that everything is reborn into: any other connected sequence is an illusion. And when you no longer believe in the illusion it's possible to actually love the life you thought was going wrong.

In the most creative sense it's the end of a fixed belief in the past and the future. Everything is always totally fresh, totally unique and spontaneous. This is the message or truth that everything is forever communicating: this is The Guiding Principle.

In a similar way to what I've just described, by using only direct experience, I enable people to dislodge their fixed beliefs. When people come to me with a strong belief that certain forces or damaging patterns are stored inside them, such as always losing money or attracting the wrong people into their lives, we embark on a search for this mysterious 'thing' supposedly lodged in their being. We look closely at what actual experiences are occurring in the present moment, because if the problem really existed *inside* them, it would be present in that moment too.

Our entire experience of life is a delivery system for the message that there is only unconditional freedom, unconditional love.

I know this can be difficult if not impossible for many to accept when we look at what's taking place in the world. For sure, there is so much pain and suffering taking place – it can appear that we are engulfed by unhappiness. Of course pain is pain and deeply unpleasant. However there is a viewpoint that offers a potential for expansion: when we are no longer identified with the stories that the mind attaches to pain – when pain is effectively drained of meaning – there is an opportunity to see a pathway leading directly to God. Without a story attached, there is a possibility to identify with the presence that pain arises in, instead of identifying solely with the pain itself. This can soften the strong resistance and sense of ownership we have to pain and create space around it. I make a point of never trying to convince anyone of anything on this front. What I'm offering is the possibility of a different viewpoint. It's one of those very delicate points of balance where there is no way to prove what is true. All I can do is offer these words with the intention to relieve suffering.

From my perspective we cause suffering and unhappiness because we become lost in a dream of separation: we believe in loss and death. Ultimately there is only the recognising of The Guiding Principle as it shapes reality, or not recognising, forgetting.

Equally hard to accept when fully identified with the mind is that Nature fully accepts both. God will wait forever in a pit of suffering and misery never ceasing to communicate the message of Unconditional Love. And in the same way, God will wait in the throws of everlasting bliss. When this is seen we can only stand in Awe.

An important question that I often get asked is:

"If what you say is true and there is only this ever-present communication of Unconditional Love, and our lives are shaped by what you call The Guiding Principle, how come I'm constantly bombarded with feelings of fear, anger, jealousy and negativity?"

The closest I am able to share as to what fundamentally happened to me on the two occasions I describe in this book, is that a powerfully rooted belief that life is 'personal' somehow evaporated. On the first occasion the shift appeared to be temporary and over time the assumption that life, events and experiences related directly to a 'personal' me regained a foothold. But on that second occasion it was realised that *the story* of "me" or the self-contraction was never actually in the way of a natural ease and non-resistance to life. Emotions and feelings were just totally accepted and left to stay or go as they pleased. At once the terrible burden of needing to control life was dropped. The burden of believing that anything was 'right' or 'wrong' died away.

This final non-resistance to life allowed me to totally see that no boundary between what appears as myself and Nature is real. And what's left is life leading directly to its own wonder or as I've termed it, The Guiding Principle giving birth to experience. It was realised that there is no reference point beyond experience itself: therefore experience can only be the touch of God, the language of God. And there is no aspect of God that we can ever be remote from.

I want to gently remind you that it's more powerful to look to where these words are pointing, rather than trying to fathom them out.

As to why someone would be bombarded with negative thoughts as opposed to positive thoughts, the first thing to recognise is that life is always living itself through us naturally no matter what is happening. Even though we may experience considerable turbulence of thoughts there is nothing 'wrong'. Life is playing out perfectly, always pointing to the truth, always delivering the message of unconditional love, regardless of whether or not it is recognised.

Remember, I finally saw the infinite radiance of life from within a pit of pain and misery. The months of utter despair had apparently stripped me down to the bone and thrown me into the purifying flames of truth. That's how it happened for me, but it can equally be seen from within the height of exaltation or any other condition. Interestingly once the radiance is seen it becomes largely irrelevant where and how the seeing took place.

Now staying with the idea of life living itself naturally, I'd like to remind you how earlier in the text I likened thoughts to weather patterns. Furthermore, we can observe that everything can be described in terms of patterns. Looking closer this even includes things that at first don't appear to form recognisable patterns such as traffic flow and people in queues. Therefore patterns appear to be an innate quality of reality: it appears to create them prolifically in every conceivable situation.

Having rekindled the analogy of thoughts being like weather patterns, I also used the term, 'environment', again in relation to thought patterns and this is a key ingredient.

To me it appears that thoughts, emotional states, forces of nature, solar flares - and all the patterns they create - occur where the environment is optimal for them to be expressed. For example, a storm begins to take shape when a center of low pressure is surrounded by a system of high pressure. In the same way that an unimaginably intricate and delicate balance of elements are needed for a thought to arise, on a bigger scale, a storm also requires a phenomenal amount of elemental interconnections in order for it to manifest.

All this translates into the observation that the correct environment needs to be present for certain weather patterns to arise and certain thought patterns to arise. Importantly both thoughts and storms are natural expressions or patterns of life, arising impersonally and spontaneously.

Unlike our ancestors most of us no longer believe storms are caused by the wrath of the Gods. Therefore despite them often causing damage, fear and considerable inconvenience, we understand they are not personally aimed at us by Nature.

So as difficult as negative thoughts are, it is possible to see that they are natural patterns arising in the environment of a mind. By the interplay of infinitely complex interactions the environment was perfect for those thought patterns to arise and fall away. Ultimately like every other aspect of Nature, certain experiences appear to occur where there is the right environment for them. And all the meanings and stories that we may attach to thoughts will never change the fact that ultimately they do not refer to a separate 'Being' set adrift in the world. No amount of searching will ever find the core of that separate 'Being'. Most of us go through our entire lives missing the simple fact that we never directly see our own face or look into our own eyes. What we are actually looking out from is the all-accepting presence of God – only God sees. And God has no separate identity and we are created in the imagination of God with no solid, separate identity. The vast wonder of who we are is always directly there, it is never hidden.

None of this is an attempt to dismiss the experience of negative or painful thoughts and feelings. Yet as with my observations on physical pain, to create an opening where the possibility of being free of the meanings and stories that we attach to thoughts, is ever-present. Without the reflex of rejection, thoughts are left to be what they are: Nature.

And as I've said, the final non-resistance to life allowed me to see that the boundary between what appears as myself and Nature is not real. And what's left is life leading directly to its own wonder or as I've termed it, The Guiding Principle. In exactly the same way, the boundary that may appear to separate you from Nature is also not real. It can immediately be seen that the space supposedly inside your body is the same as the space outside your body: both resonate at the same frequency. Investigate this for yourself.

This space is who you are: it's completely alive, vibrant and awake. The thought, 'I don't get it' appears in this 'Alive Presence' and the thought 'I'm unlucky' or 'I'm loving' also appear and disappear in this Alive Presence.

As emotions arise, no matter whether they are positive or negative, we can notice the Presence or Awareness that completely surrounds and enfolds the emotion. We can notice the labels we attach to emotions such as anger or sadness. And when an emotion arises, we can begin to see it as just raw energy that's being expressed through a mind and body: raw energy that's passing through. It has a definable beginning, middle and an end. It traces out a pattern in Presence, finally spiraling back down into the acceptance of God. All things approaching God are consumed in Her love so that the world-illuminating brilliance forever shines: God is always shinning out of and into everything from all possible perspectives.

We don't need so-called spiritual attributes or anything special for the veil which obscures Nature's brilliance to fall away. This message is not a 'spiritual' message. I'm not a spiritual teacher. In fact I was an obsessive spiritual seeker for over twenty years. Some of the practices and explorations facilitated tremendous insight and beautiful experiences. Certainly they made my life more magical and I truly honor these practices and the teachers that delivered them. And yet no matter how much I tried to sustain them, they came and went.

Each carried a particular quality that could be labeled as 'spiritual', and yet those experiences were simply birthing and dying in Presence, through the grace of The Guiding Principle. No different to the way that a dream, a swarm of bees or the lacy projection of light filtering through leaves appears in Presence. There is not one thing that's spiritual and another that's not. I feel that 'aliveness' is a far better description of what is seen to be the case once the story of 'me' is no longer believed. It describes our abundant and joyful nature that's always in service of life.

With the seeing that everything is always showing us the truth, life is accepted and fully expressed including anger, sadness and pain.

Like a hurricane, when anger has fully blown itself out, without restriction, there is calm, which is then followed by another emotion. As I've said, they appear uncensored and raw because there is no longer anything filtering them. I can even say that because emotions are known as The Guiding Principle, they are seen to communicate love. This uncensored flow of *being* becomes the 'story' instead of a separate 'me' constantly subjected to unwanted thoughts and experiences. Life is not personal, and the simple consideration of this can begin to lift the veil that appears to be separating us from God. My will is the same will that moves the clouds, the tides and the same will that throws a body face down in the mud and bathes it in dark despair.

However the crucial thing to understand is that a subtle change in the environment will create something very different. This is the same for the Sun, the wind, the mind and the body. And this is exactly what we are about to cover with the next **'Pointer'**.

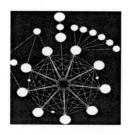

Pointer ~ 2

ALIGN WITH THE 'MESSENGERS'

Everything is always pointing to the truth, there is nothing else ever happening. This is the case for every single thing that we encounter including all the experiences we take to be us. What we perceive as time is delivering the message of truth in the same way that our words, actions and dreams deliver the same miraculous truth.

And yet despite everything pointing to the truth, the message appears stronger in some things. A beautiful flower, a stunning sunset - an inspiring work of art or words spoken with love and passion are very direct and very potent delivery systems serving The Guiding Principle.

They deliver the message that at the very core of everything there is only Unconditional Love. They show us beyond intellect that the directive of our existence is not ceaseless competition and selfishness. The Guiding Principle is a maker of love and life is the lovemaking.

By aligning ourselves with the things that most powerfully transmit the resonance of that lovemaking, an energetic shift is possible. In dropping the misconceptions and the painful stories we apply to life, a profound clarity of Being is available. I would suggest that aligning yourself with potent servants of The Guiding Principle would bring about transformation regardless of whether the story of separation was present or not: your life couldn't fail to take on a more inspired quality.

If we start to look closely at Nature we can see The Guiding Principle's signal ceaselessly directing us straight into the arms of God. Nature directly tells us what is life enhancing – I believe it's called 'the signature code'.

If we look closely at Nature we see the message of love contained in the shape and patterns of things. For example plants that are good for certain organs of the body actually look like those organs. We see that a kidney bean looks like a kidney and is in fact good for the kidneys; the ginseng root looks like a twisty little human and it energises our entire body. The Guiding Principle is constantly speaking to us, guiding us to the possibility of life being experienced and lived as a blessing.

Here is a prayer that was given to me by an old Shaman, who came to me whilst I was deep in a healing Ayahuasca journey. His features looked as if a penknife had carved them, and he had the look of such love in his eyes that all I could do was melt into that love. The prayer tells of how Nature shows us the way:

"Everyone contains the possibility to see what can be called good ~ what points towards love ~ the truth is reflected back to you in the form of things ~ it can be seen in your flesh and in the plants ~ the water ~ the clouds ~ and even in the patterns of your mind ~ still the remembering is like an infant in the arms of a mother...an infant in the arms of a mother..."

"The remembering ~ the recognition ~ is powered by your capacity to see that what you touch and what you share is only love..."

Fundamentally, we don't need any special knowledge or ability to pick up The Guiding Principle's signal: it's totally effortless and the atoms weaving us together with sound and light start to fall into harmony with the Mind of God the instant they're exposed to its truth.

In deep sleep, the transmission of truth is there: even for those lost in the patterns of pain, abuse and hatred – in the deepest silence beyond their thoughts the transmission is there. Without this constant communication life could not exist in the restriction of physical form.

In the waking state, for most of us, the message of truth is an almost imperceptible resonance emanating from the unconscious, but nevertheless it is present.

Here are some of the messengers, the most direct ways to align your energy with the powerful resonance of The Guiding Principle. There are many others and I invite you to explore and experiment.

ALIGN WITH THE MESSENGER OF

'Aliveness'

The quality of aliveness is one of the most potent and direct messengers.

Align yourself with people and things that bring aliveness to the forefront of life. Flow towards people who illuminate the world around them - people that inspire and waste no time stoking the fires of drama. The quality of aliveness has a stillness and ease at its core – it's palpable. In a sense their personalities are illuminated by aliveness, rather than constantly needing to reinforce a sense of themselves and their power in the world. They literally bring energy to life. There is a transmission of clarity around them because they've dropped the drama of past stories about what should have been different or otherwise. Their awareness is rooted in the present, fully available to life.

The fact that you recognise their aliveness and the qualities they express means that they must first be brought to life through you: you're alive with those abundant qualities. Everything that you see outside yourself is already arising out of you; otherwise there would be no recognition.

The Guiding Principle is being expressed through you as the recognition of Aliveness.

Engage in activities that evoke the experience of energy as a 'felt' quality of Aliveness flowing through your body – feel the movement of energy. Your body has the capacity to intimately know Aliveness in all its diverse and wonderful forms. Therefore dance, move, explore your sexual energy and sing instead of always talking. Singing from the heart is a bridge across the torrent of thoughts; it leads directly to the realms where transformation happens in an instant. When you do speak say things that you like the sound of: all words can create poetry when said with passion, compassion and purpose.

Aliveness is also transmitted through food. Nourishing your body with food that has recently been filled with the sun's vitality and life will evoke Aliveness in your cells. Likewise cleansing your body of toxins, removing those things that are stuck and clogging up your body's natural flow of energy, amplifies Aliveness.

Aliveness is experienced when we change our habitual ways of doing in the world, when we risk failure because it's more important to experience freshness. Remember that what we term as 'failure' is always The Guiding Principle honing us. Ultimately every failure is filled with the seeds of our transformation.

Aliveness moves in the shape of possibilities. And living from the perspective of possibility makes our minds supple and able to bend to the changes life gifts to us. It makes us ripe for transformation in the knowing that it is always good.

Aliveness delivers what can be called true abundance because it amplifies the truth in us all. When your heart is rich with Aliveness, the richness of your experience is true wealth.

Live through the raw, actual sensory experiencing itself rather than the stories you attach to experiences: aliveness is free of conditions and judgments.

ALIGN WITH THE MESSENGER OF

'Creativity'

We are all innately creative. And yet so many of us learn to ignore or deny this natural gift. Creativity is simply the bringing into being of something that did not exist before. It is a merging of energies and ideas that have not previously merged.

Regardless of whether or not we are aware of it, we are constantly engaged in this process: we voyage into the non-linear realm of symbols and metaphors to gather the raw ingredients of manifestation. In this way creativity is far more than a function of mind, it's more like an enhanced faculty to bring what is hidden into view. Art and music for example have tremendous power to expose the miracle of life waiting to be discovered in the perceived shadows as well as the joy of our life stories.

We are immersed daily in the most incredible outpouring of creativity and invention. It could be said that this is the **Age of Creativity** and that we are living in extraordinary times with unimaginable opportunities for creative adventure.

Creativity gives us the ability to see ourselves from an expanded and far more open perspective. Our creations reveal and reflect back hitherto undiscovered facets of life and ourselves. Creativity actively demonstrates that life spontaneously emerges into being.

Importantly, creativity doesn't wait for us to believe in it to be expressed: that's why it's such a powerful servant of The Guiding Principle. It brings us directly into contact with the possibility that every single aspect of life is being guided by an unimaginably vast intelligence. And yet creativity can be found in the very smallest of acts such as preparing food, asking a question or simply doing something differently.

Try drawing when thinking through an issue instead of writing about it. Much of the time when we communicate with words, the language shrinks the infinite down to limited forms. The freedom of creativity once again expands us into the possibility of infinity. If you're upset, pour your heart out completely uncensored in shapes and colours. Allow the emotions to be fully expressed in a totally unique way. This has nothing do with so-called 'High Art', but rather it's connecting with our raw creative natures.

Look for answers to life's questions in Nature – notice what She lays on the path before you. These processes will move you past the mind's compulsion to neutralise, figure out, overcome or get rid of. You will uncover the wisdom of Nature: The Guiding Principle will gradually reveal its mind, the Mind of God.

Creativity is Nature at play, laughing through itself at itself. It is a holistic realm where we can join things together, make sense of and bring healing to our experiences. We catch a glimpse of the whole picture and see how everything is connected.

Simply recognising and expressing your own creativity and aligning with other forms of creativity will automatically harmonise you with The Guiding Principle. A direct energetic recognition beyond the mind, beyond concepts is available.

Live through the raw, actual sensory experiencing of creativity as you bring yourself into greater and greater alignment with its natural expression. Everything we imagine is Nature imagining. Everything we see and feel is Nature seeing and feeling. And in the most obvious and direct way the neurons in our brain do not fire at the bidding of any separate presence or entity. They are Nature unconditionally giving birth to a mind that can never be owned by anything, not even God.

In a mire of rules and conditioning we cannot see that the power of The Guiding Principle is always alive and fully expressed through everything that we experience. Creativity is mysteriously like a remembering of this.

As the old, gnarled Shaman's prayer said:

"The remembering ~ the recognition ~ is powered by your capacity to see that what you touch and what you share is only love…"

ALIGN WITH THE MESSENGER OF

'Beauty'

If we closely observe the experience of beauty we notice that it is not objective: it doesn't exist *inside* anything. This is why it's possible to find someone or something beautiful at one time, and no longer perceive that beauty on another occasion. This is a very common experience. It can feel as if the beauty has mysteriously drained away. The person we found so intoxicatingly beautiful turns out to be selfish or unreliable and suddenly we no longer find them beautiful. Or a place that we found so beautiful as a child, upon revisiting, turns out to be nothing special.

If beauty existed inside people, objects, places or even thoughts it would always be present, a ceaseless quality no matter what. As we've already explored, everything is totally empty, therefore aligning with the transmission of beauty simply involves noticing when it is present in your own raw experience rather than seeing it as something residing in people or things.

As with Aliveness and Creativity, Beauty is a potent delivery system. And as with the other strong messengers of truth, it delivers the brilliance of Nature or God directly through our sensory perceptions.

Beauty is the recognition that we are ultimately unlimited: it evokes a knowing of this. And like the elaborate plumage of the male peacock, the experience of beauty immediately draws our attention: it literally announces the self-radiant presence of God. And whilst the experience of beauty is happening the objective world is temporarily illuminated: we see the light-trail left by The Guiding Principle. Beauty could be said to be an expression of harmony, elegance and balance, the natural order of things – fresh and innocent, raw and vital. When we cultivate beauty the world is revitalised. Beauty brings things back to life.

Always…the raw experience of beauty as it arises will reveal The Guiding Principle at play with reality. It allows you to know that the Universe cannot be made of a dead substance and therefore you cannot be made out of a dead substance. The fact that you have the capacity to recognise the transmission of beauty means that this quality is alive in existence – your existence. Beauty is being expressed through you in this moment.

ALIGN WITH THE MESSENGER OF

'Intelligence'

Our culture has become fixated with the function or mechanics of intelligence. We have dreamt up ways of supposedly measuring intelligence, such as IQ (Intelligence Quotient) tests. All this is fine but it completely misses the simple fact that these tests tell us nothing about what makes something intelligent, what gives something intelligence.

However, if we examine the raw experience – what intelligence feels like – we can begin to notice that it possesses a certain quality. And this quality is alive for everyone.

Intelligence arises independently of thinking. Its manifestation in experience creates a particular luminosity. We even label so-called intelligent people as 'bright' and those who appear to possess an abundance of intelligence as 'brilliant'. This is no coincidence because it points to our ability to recognise intelligence as a quality of experience rather than purely a capacity. In the grip of convention we simply forget to look beyond function.

Our ability to recognise the quality of intelligence is good news for people like myself who can't answer most of the IQ-type questions. So despite not being able to add up even simple sets of numbers or work out a single solution on most crosswords, I can fully experience the flow of intelligence: I can know intelligence in the most intimate way.

This is because intelligence moves through us – through our minds - illuminating neurons, bringing certain things to light in our minds, leading to our ability to perceive connections. Intelligence moves through our hearts illuminating love and compassion. And it moves through other parts of our bodies illuminating a greater elegance of movement and wellbeing. Intelligence is an experienced quality of The Guiding Principle that moves our being towards greater and greater harmony with Nature.

We perceive the quality of intelligence as it illuminates our minds, our hearts and our physical structures. And to know intelligence in this way opens us to the possibility of seeing exactly what's needed.

I invite you to play with recognising the quality of intelligences in yourself and other people. See how certain types of intelligence such as intellectual, emotional and physical intelligence shine out in yourself and others. Experiment by connecting with others who appear to emit brightness in a particular area that you don't immediately see in yourself.

By aligning with these four messengers: Aliveness, Creativity, Beauty and Intelligence you create an environment where The Guiding Principle can be experienced as it is presently happening. There is no need to work hard at them or take them too seriously; just enjoy exploring them and noticing what your experience is from moment to moment. It's amazing just how willingly The Guiding Principle reveals its brilliance to us when we enter into a playful relationship with life. We come to realise that it was always right there in every aspect of our life – moving us to the truth of who we are.

Opening ~ Three

THERE IS NO DISTANCE BETWEEN YOU

AND THE GUIDING PRINCIPLE

No Distance Between You and The Mind of God

All you ever need in order to connect with The Guiding Principle on the most intimate level imaginable is your direct experience. All you ever need to do is realise that you are having an experience, whatever that experience may be, and you will know The Guiding Principle. What you see, what you hear and what you feel is never for one instant separate. There is not a single piece of evidence that anything can exist independent of experience. This is why we don't need the unfathomable complexity of mathematics or science to extend our senses. Science is amazing and very useful, however we have learnt to surrender our innate capacity of knowing the truth to disciplines such as science and technology.

I don't understand the complexities of science and yet I intimately know the Mind of God. I know the mind of God so well because it is the very experience that I'm having right now. You know the Mind of God because it is totally inseparable from the experience that you are having right now. This is fundamentally what was seen on the day that I collapsed face down in the mud: and again as I opened the car door.

There is no mysterious energy journeying out from us to make contact with a separate, external world. At first this is difficult to accept because we are constantly told that we have to place our attention on things. And we, as separate entities, very convincingly appear to affect things in an external world. This creates the belief that some kind of arbitrating energy beams out from our head or eyes to unite us with objects. However, if we look at the moon, it appears immediately and inseparably as the experience of seeing the moon. The moon and the perceived 'me' looking at the moon are always one and the same. And as we look at someone we love, the one we love and the seeing of them are one and the same.

As you look at the one you love, you are looking directly from Presence. If you move closer, they become bigger and bigger in your vision: this happens instantaneously in Presence. Eventually if you draw closer they fill your entire field of vision until there is just a blur of colours. Then if you had the capacity to journey further in, you would move through skin, cells, atoms and eventually arrive back at Presence – right where the experience emanates from: there was never any distance. The Presence waiting at the supposed end of the one you love is *you*.

When first realised, this can appear strange or even alarming for some. Yet it will eventually give rise to boundless joy because it leads to the awareness that we cannot be separate from God, we are never separate from God.

Remember, there's no need to try and understand any of this intellectually. Right now you can notice that as you look at something – this book perhaps – the book can never be separate from the experience of seeing the book. As you hold this book in your hands, what appears as the feel of a book cannot be separated from the experience of feeling. Feeling and what is felt describe the same thing: there is no gap between them. Distance is actually a quality projected onto reality by our senses.

Until we investigate and come to see that what is experienced and experiencing are identical, our senses effectively disguise the utter intimacy and interconnectedness of reality. And as the belief in separation gently falls away all that's left is the true nature of Nature. Again we discover that the Universe is vibrantly alive and we are the same vibrant aliveness. We are the ever-accepting Presence and The Guiding Principle weaving the threads of experiences together.

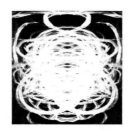

Pointer ~ 3

Feel into the direct experience you are having right now.

After reaching this point, I wasn't sure how to talk about the next Opening and Pointer to The Guiding Principle.

I left the book alone and carried on with my life.

A week passed and I still had nothing to say. Then one afternoon I felt drawn to have a look through some artworks stored inside a cupboard in my office. I opened the door and a small black sketchbook leapt out and dropped to the floor. I picked it up noticing it had fallen open at a page with a single sentence written in blue ink. I remembered writing this sentence many years ago.

I carefully placed the book back. However, the next day when I walked into my office the cupboard door was open and a whole bunch of things were strewn across the floor. The sketchbook was amongst the different items. I picked it up and saw it had fallen open at the same page as before. Once again I read the simple sentence. Of course I had a feeling that it was telling me something, but at first I couldn't see how this old sketchbook and a few simple words were relevant. Then as I thought about the events leading up to my writing the words I suddenly understood.

This absolutely wasn't how I expected to arrive at the final Opening and Pointer. But The Guiding Principle doesn't require us to follow any set rules or conventions.

This is what I need to share with you…

Opening ~ Four

THE SHADOW

At thirty-three I was pretty disenchanted with life. This was nothing like the end-point I experienced at forty-four, but nonetheless it was unpleasant.

For me disenchantment is when the possibility of wonder drains out of life, and we find ourselves stuck in a world that no longer contains the capacity to inspire.

My design and media business had fallen into a creative and financial abyss, and I spent my days locked in meetings with dreary moneymen talking about rescue packages. I trudged through the motions wondering why I couldn't care less what happened.

In truth I didn't really have far to look for an answer. My spiritual practices such as meditation and studying shamanism had more or less ground to a halt. Long cherished dreams that had once seemed so bright and aerodynamic were falling in tatters like butterflies laced with napalm. I was totally burnt out creatively and my hairline was receding as quickly as my imagination. And if that wasn't enough, I was drinking so much red wine that my local shop already had the bottle on the counter as soon as I walked in.

Early one morning before the normal round of mind-numbing meetings, I sat in my studio staring at the company credit card, wondering how long before the bank demanded it back. The whole situation felt like the films where a soldier is dishonorably discharged from the cavalry: medals and stripes ceremonially ripped off, thrown to the ground and trampled into the dust.

The platinum credit card is of course a kind of trick medal pinned to a uniform we call 'success'. However, sitting innocently on my desk it now seemed to contain a blurry promise that I couldn't quite bring into focus.

As I sat trying to decode the strange new resonance encrypted into the card, the phone rang. I picked it up knowing it was my call to yet another meeting with the accountants and a potential buyer of my business. I had met this potential buyer a few times before. And on each occasion had the immediate feeling that I would rather go down in flames, than hand him a company which had given birth to so much creative innovation.

It wasn't so much that I didn't like this man, although I can't say he appeared to be blessed with an abundance of endearing qualities. No...it was more to do with allowing my business - something that had shone so brightly - to die with dignity.

The potential buyer had plans to graft us onto his trading company. We would effectively be put out to grass designing annual reports and media presentations with the usual fake smiles and massaged accounts. As a once *enfant terrible* of the design world, this was exactly what I had spent years rebelling against. How on earth had I ended up here? The whole situation felt like a world champion boxer who winds up fighting bare-knuckled in dirty alleyways for a few shots of cheap gin.

I put the phone down and didn't make any attempt to move. Something about the credit card still drew my attention. I picked it up and twirled it between my fingers before putting it back down. I then found myself picking up the phone and dialing my accountant's number. I heard myself telling him that I wouldn't be attending the meeting. Furthermore, I continued, the business was no longer for sale and I intended to cease trading.

I could almost feel the colour draining out of his face. He was most likely already locked into the normal round of polite insincerities that characterised so much of conventional business.

Sliding the credit card back into my wallet, I left the studio and walked to a small park just around the corner. Suddenly the world felt more spacious. It was as if I'd been trapped in a broom cupboard and only just realised that all I had to do was open the door and leave. I switched off my phone and sat in the park for the rest of the day watching squirrels raiding the bins.

Later on that evening I was having dinner with Esther, who was then my girlfriend. It was rare for me to be home before midnight. Over the past few months, she had kept me going, preparing delicious food and massaging my shoulders when they seemed to be carrying the weight of the world. She had also been instrumental in diffusing the operatic drama that seemed to be part of my DNA in those days. To this day the numerous acts of kindness, support, wisdom, creativity and healing that Esther gifts to the world on an average day is really quite astounding.

Anyway, after dinner she disappeared into the next room and returned with a large picture book. The book was filled with stunning images of Mexico, in particular some absolutely mesmerising art from the Huichol tribe, direct descendants of the Aztecs.

My eyes danced over the images and there was nothing to be said. The blurry promise encrypted into my credit card had just come sharp into focus.

Knowing I had to act very quickly, first thing the next morning I booked two plane tickets to Mexico. Next I sprinted to the nearest cash machine. Holding my breath as I keyed in the PIN, I requested the maximum amount possible. The machine seemed to recognise that I was up to something, but after several suspicious noises it finally released the money. The banks had just unwittingly financed an adventure.

I felt a bit like a fugitive, except I was on the run from being reasonable. When life moves us it has no concern for our human constructs of reason and practicalities: we just have to go. So over the next few days, moved by a power that I had no name for, I became completely deaf to the often-angry monologues from business associates and various representatives urgently sent from the bank.

However, one thing I did do pertaining to 'reasonable', was set aside some of the money I had syphoned out of the credit card, to pay a few designers that I still owed money to. Even so, the final act of paying them must have looked more like a gangland drug deal than payment for creative design work. I arranged to meet the small clutch of designers in a nearby pub. It was the days before smoking had been banned, and this was the kind of pub only frequented by serious drinkers and smokers. We sat engulfed in clouds of cigarette smoke, and much to the designers' astonishment, I handed over bags of cash instead of the rubber cheques they were most likely expecting.

I understood that I would probably have to face the tax gallows for negligence when I returned home from Mexico, but for the first time in ages I actually felt alive. Handing over the bags of money felt like an act of love and respect - to hell with the tax office and the banks.

The next few days flew by in a haze of preparation and fending off more objections. So it wasn't until I found myself sitting next to Esther on the plane that I suddenly realised how exhausted I was. Only then did I begin to consider the fact that I was virtually bankrupt and no longer had a company: moreover, who was I without it? The months of intense stress and despondency had also taken its toll on my health: I felt considerably older than thirty-three, and probably looked it too.

As we flew towards Mexico I drifted in and out of uneasy dreams. I couldn't quite grasp what they were about, but these dreamy segues largely seemed to feature a large orange snake, and to my surprise, an Italian man that I had briefly known many years ago, when I was an art student. He called himself Dal, possibly short for Dalmazio. He never divulged his actual name.

We had originally met in a record shop called 'Rough Trade' in London's Covent Garden. I was clutching a book called 'The Doors of Perception' by Aldous Huxley, detailing his experiences with the hallucinogenic substance, Mescaline. I'd only read a few opening pages and had a quick flick through. It seemed quite dense and I was largely carrying it for show.

Unaware of my wish to appear mature and intellectual, the book immediately attracted Dal's attention. The ensuing conversation revealed our shared fascination for things arty, shamanic and multidimensional.

I wasn't exactly ordinary in terms of style, but Dal was on a planet of his own. He was a proto punk rocker in his mid thirties, covered from head to toe in a complex matrix of tribal tattoos, and still sporting a turquoise Mohican. He normally wore clothes such as leopard skin jackets and PVC bondage pants.

He was a cluster of contradictions - mostly challenging and chaotic. Yet underneath the maelstrom of image and activity, he was a sensitive questioner of reality and sometimes wise when least expected.

One day I was complaining about something going wrong, when he just looked up from a book he was flicking through and said: *"Davide, there are no mistakes in the world and no one will ever understand you."* These words completely took the wind out of my sails and I made a point of never complaining in his company again.

On another occasion when I met him in a pub, he was already engaged in a conversation with a young woman who was clearly angry. She completely ignored me so I didn't bother to introduce myself. I'm not entirely sure what they were talking about but suddenly she bellowed out, "You have to be responsible!" People in the pub began staring at our table.

Instead of reacting, Dal simply looked her directly in the eyes and in a very soft and calm voice said:

"There is no such thing as responsibility...we've all been poisoned by this idea...we're not even responsible for our own birth or the construction of the brain sitting in our heads. When we're free of this bullshit idea called responsibility, then maybe we can just naturally take care of each other when life leads us to do so. Without all these rules we can see life more clearly. And without faith or hope we can see the impossibility of death."

The young woman wasn't at all happy with his response because she grabbed her things and stormed out of the pub. However, for me, something in those words resonated on a very deep level. They struck me as an odd response to what appeared to be a domestic dispute, but then again Dal wasn't the sort of person to let ordinary life get in the way of philosophical exploration.

Although I didn't know it back then, life was already chipping away at my conditioning. I also didn't know it would take another twenty-five years, along with countless up's and down's, to actually realise why those words seemed to point towards the truth.

On top of everything else, Dal was the first person I met who had smoked the mystical substance DMT – often termed the 'spirit molecule' - and the active ingredient in the shamanic medicine, Ayahuasca. And to my eyes back then - the eyes of a nineteen-year-old art student - Dal represented the possibility of never succumbing to the gravitational pull of convention.

We lost touch when Dal returned to Italy after a rather mysterious brush with the law. He left in a hurry without so much as a simple goodbye. I never found out quite what happened, but assumed his exodus had something to do with the abundance of marijuana he normally carried around with him. He would freely hand it out and always had plenty of money to spend on records and clothes. He certainly didn't do anything even vaguely resembling a job, yet he lived in a plush apartment in South London. So rightly or wrongly, I assumed he was some kind of dealer. We never had a conversation about it though: instead our time was spent in the realms of art, music, esoteric literature and science fiction.

Just before he left, we met at Camden Market in North-West London. Dal handed me a postcard with the words, *'We are all miraculously out of control'* in big black type on one side and the words, *'Beliefs aren't necessary'* on the other. It made me smile.

So when Dal materialised in my dreams on the plane, I took it to be symbolic of my refusal to hand over my business to the corporate suits. His sudden and unexpected appearance had bothered me for a day or so after arriving in Mexico, but once Esther and I started our travels, the dreams were more or less forgotten. However I found it difficult to forget the tatters my life appeared to be in. Almost immediately I developed a kind of foggy headache accompanied by a mild fever.

Much to my relief, Esther was a brilliant navigator. This was fortunate because for the most part I had practically no idea where we were going and was more or less useless. The fog swirling around in my head made me feel as if I was always heading towards an unseen precipice. It was almost impossible to relax and on several occasions we had to stop traveling until this feeling subsided.

Nevertheless after a couple of weeks I began to feel much more at ease. We delighted in the mysterious temples and pyramids, awash with the sacred geometries, magic and the art of the Mayan, Toltec and Aztec cultures. We also connected with contemporary artists, musicians and other creative adventurers like ourselves. This infused our trip with a sense of aliveness and new discovery. In such a stimulating mix I even began to feel a stirring of fun and optimism. The simmering hornet's nest of debt and unfinished business awaiting my return to London seemed like another lifetime.

After traveling through Mexico for a few weeks, our attention shifted to Guatemala, located off the Southern tip of Mexico. Originally we had no plans to go there, but after hearing many stories of its beauty from other travelers – particularly the active volcanoes, the indigenous tribal peoples and a vast tropical forest – we decided to go. In our enthusiasm we somehow managed to miss the descriptions of some of the incredible violence that sadly afflicts this amazing country.

Even without this information, almost as soon as we started moving towards Guatemala, I felt a dramatic shift in mood. The same head-fog that had plagued me right at the start of our trip returned. And as we journeyed towards the boarder crossing, both Dal and the large orange snake made a powerful and unwanted comeback.

Almost every night in a dream, I would find myself in a crummy room. It seemed to be somewhere in a densely urban part of London, but I couldn't make out where. The carpet and furniture were moth-eaten and it stank of neglect. At first the sun was always shinning outside. But before I had a chance to register what was happening, an eerie, spectral twilight instantly replaced the bright sunshine. I would run to the decrepit, finger-smeared window to see what had happened.

Pulling the window open, splinters of fossilized paint would fall in slow motion to the ground below. I had the feeling that a total eclipse was looming above, as a chilling hush poured over everything like liquid silence. Next the sky would always fill with thick crimson clouds before turning pitch black. Outside none of the street lamps were working, and there was not a single person or car to be seen anywhere.

At this point Dal would enter the room. I was both pleased and relieved to see him. That was until I noticed he was carrying a huge orangey snake. I've never been the slightest bit scared of snakes: I actually find them amazing creatures. And yet in this context it was overwhelming.

As if that wasn't enough, Dal would quite joyfully set the snake down near my feet. But thinking that it may be poisonous I would try and edge past it.

Dal would look me directly in the eyes. *"Davide, don't be afraid,"* he would say in his tuneful Italian accent. *"It's impossible for anything that appears in dreams or life to go against what you most need."*

He would then smile. *"You need to follow it,"* he would say.

And upon the utterance of those words, the snake would start sliding towards the door. Yet despite being curious I wasn't about to follow it. Instead I watched as it reached the boot-scuffed door and slid underneath. The whole scenario carried the malignant ambiance of a nightmare.

However, one night, whilst still dreaming, I took a close look at the snake. And to my great surprise it was remarkably beautiful. Rather than just the dull orange I had always seen, the skin was decorated with the most intricate, interlacing fractal patterns which were truly hypnotic and looked incredibly familiar: I just couldn't place where I had seen them.

It took a few more nights of Dal and the snake for me to realise that the markings resembled the delicate beadwork found on the ceremonial masks made by the Huichol Indians. This one connection had the affect of completely neutralising the sinister quality of the dreams. Of course I understood that something was happening - I just didn't know what. Now it seemed kind of obvious that someone like Dal would be a dream messenger. The more I thought about it, he was also covered with patterns. He was a piece of human Huichol art.

Esther had carried some small books on the Huichol people all the way from London. So as we crossed over into Guatemala on an old 1950's high school bus, I started to document the dreams and also read more about the Huichol. It turned out the name Huichol was derived from another word, Wirrarika, their original name. This original name means 'soothsayer' or 'medicine man'.

With my imagination sparked, as we journeyed towards the tropical forest, I started to think about the symbolism of snakes in dreams. Of course there was the obvious association with the phallus, which I didn't feel I could completely ignore. But there were also other interpretations such as the snake's connection to the shadow worlds because of its amazing ability to live within the dark realms of the earth. The snake also emerges from the shadows to embrace light flowing from the sun. The snake's ability to populate both light and dark encapsulates the ancient sorcerers nature of moving in perfect rhythm with the natural forces.

I knew that alchemical texts were also full of snake symbols. This was interesting and I started to delve into the snake symbol a step further, looking at the serpent connection to the creation or transformation of life and the formation of DNA. My thoughts drifted to how information traveling through our minds is now systematically becoming electricity traveling through silicon. I had read that information would soon be stored in nothing more than pure light. Maybe it was propelling the whole of our consciousness towards a kind of 'spiritual technology' where we would finally create our own version of immortality?

On the seemingly endless bus journeys, my mind drifted on and on into ever more obscure imaginings. Sleep came easily and Dal drifted into dream existence like a ghost becoming corporeal. In these new dreams the nasty, urban room had transformed into a garden of living rocks. The snake had also transformed, now taking the form of the sacred Peyote cactus, depicted in much of the Huichol peoples' art: this seemed significant.

The ecstasy and visions given by the Peyote cactus are really the vital energies which give birth to the sacred artworks. And for the people who see the cactus as a direct link to God, there can be no art without their religion or religion without their art. Religion is not a mere aspect of life: it's the very essence of life. They know their gods are everywhere including the trees, mountains and lakes. All of life is vitalised and even the rocks and stones posses a soul. Living in a vast city it's easy to lose sight of the fact that everything must first be granted reality, and the power which grants reality cannot be anywhere except in the things it creates.

This reminded me of an ancient saying...

God Sleeps in the Stone

God Dreams in the Plant

God moves in the Animals

And God Awakens in Us

In one of the last dreams that Dal appeared in, we had a conversation. I kept a record of the dream in my sketchbook. I wouldn't truly know the power of these words for many years to come.

Sitting on a living rock in the garden, telluric energy poured up from the earth and into my body.

"Dal, what are you doing here?" I asked.

He looked at me with real kindness in his eyes. *"I discovered that we never go anywhere except in our imagination,"* he replied.

Then, seeming to pick up a distant signal, he continued: *"You're scared of life right now, but all you have to remember is that every experience that you have has first been bathed in the unconditional love of God."*

I studied him carefully, noticing that the tattoos on his arms were Huichol art. I didn't remember them like this. I didn't remember him quite like this at all.

I sensed that he hadn't finished his last sentence and somehow in the dream I knew what he wanted to say.

"Every experience is simply the after-glow of that first miracle," I heard myself say. They weren't my words but it wasn't important.

We laughed together. *"When you think you're the one moving your life, Davide, the beauty of life is always invisible,"* said Dal, picking up a stone. *"We don't own anything, not our bodies, not our minds."*

I wanted to ask about the snake but simply couldn't find the words.

I watched him throw the stone into the air. At that point the dream faded...

And so our journey through Guatamala continued. The roads steadily became dirt tracks as the rain forest enveloped us in its verdant body. Simply being in the awesome energy of such a great forest was a humbling experience. The ceaseless aliveness of Nature was ever apparent: everything dancing to the music of life. The hot and moist air drifted into the bus licking our flesh like the tongue of a great nature spirit. This whole place was water exploring what it's like to have eyes, a brain and legs.

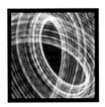

Eventually the old high school bus could go no further, and we had to make our way through the forest on foot to a small village that we hoped could accommodate us. With my still nonexistent sense of direction and ropey Spanish, we would probably still be wandering that forest. Mercifully Esther's natural homing device was still going strong, and just as our backpacks were feeling more like houses and darkness was beginning to descend, we spotted the village.

We were accompanied all the way by the mournful song of large, jet-black Howler monkeys in the canopy above. This definitely sounded more like a lament than a welcome. I had visions of us being turned away as unwelcome intruders and spending the night wandering lost in the forest.

Fortunately though the villagers were quite friendly, but at the same time tough and direct. It was obvious that they had seen their fair share of hardship and violence over the years. Their personalities were carved fresh from nature's chisel each morning. There simply wasn't time or need for smooth edges. I remember thinking that we must seem quite alien to them with our manicured, London behavior.

After what felt like way too long, it was agreed that we would stay in a house owned by a man with a face like an old and twisted vine. A small clay pipe was permanently grafted to his lower lip, and a great deal of his attention was focused on keeping this tiny burner primed and stoked.

To our surprise he led us back out of the village and along a winding path that appeared to be going nowhere. But after about five minutes we arrived in a small clearing populated by a single ramshackle hut; mostly made of rusty corrugated iron. Esther and

I stared in disbelief, fighting off giant mosquitoes, whilst the vine-faced man prized open the rusty door and proudly motioned for us to take a look inside. The Howler monkeys cried mournfully just as I peered inside and I took their lament as a bad omen. The rancid smell inside the shack took my breath away. I quickly withdrew my head and smiled at the vine-faced man, searching out the words for 'do you have anywhere else' in Spanish.

As the terrible smell floated out from the open door, Esther had the same thought but a different approach, forcefully shaking her head from side to side. This seemed to trigger a strong reaction in the vine-faced man and he launched into a completely unintelligible and nonsensical stream of words and gesticulations. The man's face was so characterised that it was almost impossible to make out if he was smiling or scowling.

Finally, none the wiser, we all set off back to the village, Esther flatly refusing to set foot in such a dirty and unloved abode. Of course she was absolutely right, basic was no problem, but unloved and dirty was a different matter. However upon our return to the village a different nonsensical flow of words began to unfold. This one involved Esther, the vine-faced man, a much older woman - abundantly decorated with silver earrings and necklaces, a very young man with an oil-stained vest, a woman cradling a baby in her arms and another woman who I guessed was married to the vine-faced man.

For the first time since leaving home, I actually found myself hankering after a boring meeting with the accountants. I wondered how easy it would be to rekindle the aborted sale once I returned home.

Meanwhile, Esther had somehow managed to orchestrate the viewing of another house, much to the now very obvious displeasure of the vine-faced man. So picking up our backpacks again, we trudged off along another path following the woman clutching the baby. This path flowed into another small clearing with a far more lovingly attended corrugated shack in the middle. This one even had flowers hanging outside. Esther and the woman were smiling and laughing together: thank God for women!

Apparently dinner had also been arranged and as night descended we sat munching on fresh and pungent bread with bean-like side dishes. The ethereal symphony of frogs and other night creatures seemed to be everywhere at once: it was total sensory immersion.

After we'd eaten, I busied myself clearing the shack of unwanted insects and rigged up the mosquito net. At last we slid into a surprisingly comfortable bed and were asleep in seconds.

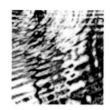

I can't remember if it was the water pouring onto our heads or the ear-shattering noise that woke us up. I fumbled under my pillow for the torch, and as our eyes adjusted to the light, we realised that we were in the middle of a violent tropical storm. The ear-shattering noise was rain pounding onto the corrugated roof. The shack wasn't exactly rainproof and dozens of mini cascades were poring in through the metal sheets above our heads.

Shinning the torch around, I saw that the room had become a haven for every conceivable insect, mostly mosquitoes. Nevertheless we both braved the onslaught of bites and stings to heave the bed across the room to a semi-dry spot. Thankfully the storm quickly died down and once again the forest resumed its ethereal symphony.

We were just dozing off when a loud smashing sound sent me once again groping for the torch. This time it wasn't the weather. We sat up in bed listening to what could only be someone walking across the roof. Every so often there was an ear-splitting smash just outside the door. Then just to add to the mix, someone or something started tugging at the door. Fortunately I'd firmly bolted it, but whoever was tugging away outside had so much power that I seriously thought the whole shack would come crashing down around our ears.

By now we were both up and fully dressed as pots began to fall off the shelves. I quickly liberated a hunting knife that I'd stored in my backpack. I had all sorts of images running through my mind. But before I could fix on any of them, we heard the grunts that could only be monkeys and of course it suddenly made sense.

I reluctantly put on my boots and went outside. But to my surprise I found no trace of any monkeys. I assumed they had fled when they heard me opening the door. (I would subsequently discover that Howler monkeys would never normally do such a thing. They are amongst the least active monkeys and normally sleep soundly at night).

With the situation resolved, we both climbed back into bed completely exhausted. I kept the torch on for a bit, but we must have dozed off because all was peaceful when I woke up needing to relieve myself. So reluctantly, yet again I left the sanctuary of the mosquito net, put on a pair of shorts and tugged on my boots. As I stepped outside, the air itself resonated with the white noise of aliveness. I felt as if I had walked into a deeply private space reserved exclusively for creatures and insects. Pockets of silence proceeded my footsteps like tiny meditation zones, and the extravagant structures of the forest seemed to worship each miniature portal to stillness.

I relieved myself and instead of going straight back in, stood marveling at the profusion of plants and sounds. Suddenly I dropped the torch and heard it hit the floor. The light immediately went out and I was struck by just how incredibly pitch black it was without this small light-source. Even as my eyes adjusted I could only pick out vague shapes in the darkness.

I retrieved the torch and tried to switch it back on but it didn't respond. I shook it and thankfully the light flickered before resurrecting itself. It was then that I completely froze. Entwined on a branch right in front of my eyes, almost touching my head was a large brown snake. Sadly it wasn't covered in the same beautiful patterns as the one in my dreams, but we were literally staring straight into each other's eyes.

It's strange what goes through the mind when faced with danger. Instead of considering the pros and cons of being bitten by a poisonous snake, I found myself wondering how a human was perceived through reptilian senses. What did the snake make of this human animal?

Even though the snake wasn't a piece of tribal art, I felt this encounter was the very thing I'd been moving towards. It seemed ironic that after all the journeying and all the dreams, this was actually it. All I had to do now was follow where it went. However this was the bit I wasn't sure about: part of me still thought it was totally crazy. How could there possibly be any real connection between the dreams and what was happening now? And yet, at the same time, I had always delighted in the exploration of art and all things wild and wonderful. It was that deeper, freer part of me that believed there was a connection: it was this part which stopped me running away and forgetting the whole thing.

I very gently backed away to what I thought was a safe distance and waited for the snake to make a move. I kept the torch trained on it as we continued to weigh each other up for quite a while. Again I started to doubt my instinct; maybe I really was deluding myself. Perhaps the dreams about a snake covered in sacred art were nothing more than a stress-related fantasy? It occurred to me that considering the loss of my business and the state of my finances, maybe I should reconsider the phallus connection, instead of some kind of sacred mission. But before I had time to journey deeper into these thoughts, the snake started to move.

It gracefully disentwined itself from the branch and descended the tree. Touching down on the forest floor, it paused. It seemed to be searching for some kind of signal or directive, independent of its own nature. It coiled its body into a spiral, then suddenly appeared to tune into something tangible: off it went at a ridiculously fast pace with me in hot pursuit.

The torch started to flicker as I chased after the snake and I was annoyed with myself for being careless with it: a torch is a very valuable tool in the rain forest. But as I continued after the snake, the unsteady beam of light began to fade and there was of course no time to go and collect another torch. In the darkness I was blindly walking into all kinds of unpleasant web-like structures. There was no point to even try and continue, it looked as if I had been deluding myself after all, this was leading nowhere.

Aside from feeling all sorts of things brushing against my face, I was also getting badly bitten by mosquitoes and I could feel the itchy welts erupting on my calves, shoulders and arms. This was not the right time to be rummaging through a tropical forest in a vest and a pair of shorts.

With a last glimmer of hope, I reached into my pocket and rummaged around for the cigarette lighter I sometimes carried. It was probably in my other trousers, but to my surprise I found it and quickly flicked it on.

In spite of the dreams, I hadn't exactly been prepared for the snake, but now I was even less prepared to find myself staring straight at a Howler monkey. Its jet-black face and lavish fur momentarily sparkled with gold in the sudden glow of the lighter flame. Shocked, I instantly dropped the lighter and we were both plunged into total darkness.

I imagined that being bitten by one of these monkeys could easily land me in hospital: that is, if there was a hospital to land in. I didn't know one way or the other if they were aggressive, nevertheless, I didn't want to increase my chances of finding out.

I experienced a sudden rush of fear, but was determined to stay calm. It wasn't hard to guess that the monkey had far better night sight than me. All I could do was fumble around, but suddenly had the thought to give the dead torch one last try. It took me three goes but at last I had the weakest of light beams.

Hesitantly I shone the light ahead of me, and to my dismay the monkey was right where I last saw it, worse still, there were now four others.

It suddenly struck me that after all the stress and months of seemingly endless attempts to save my business, I was to end my days in a dark and distant forest. If it wasn't the snake, then maybe the monkeys and if not them, there was probably something else waiting to complete the job. This thought suddenly struck me as hilarious and I started to laugh out loud. And so, for a short time, the tropical orchestra was drowned out by laughter. The more I thought about the images of me chasing after snakes and now facing a troop of monkeys in the dark, the more I had to laugh.

For some unknown reason the sound of me laughing seemed to agitate the monkeys and this just made me laugh more. I didn't even attempt to move away when one of the monkeys edged closer. I now saw the monkeys through the eyes of laughter and knew beyond thought that they were completely harmless. My shift in energy was the subtle and instant signal for them to leave. And again I would later discover that this kind of behavior from Howler monkeys was totally unheard of. On explaining this episode to local people they would look at me as if I had gone completely insane.

Nevertheless, as the monkeys danced off into the trees, the feint little beam of light from the torch illuminated something on the forest floor, just where the first monkey had been standing. I walked over and picked it up, and in the dim light I could make out that it was a piece of turquoise stone about the size and shape of a very small bird's egg. It was difficult to tell if it had been fashioned by hand or simply worn into that shape by the elements. Bringing it right up to the light I saw that it was flecked with an array of gold veins. The possibility that it had once been part of an exquisite necklace or bracelet crossed my mind. For a brief moment, it became a piece of treasure, an ancient healing serpent made of turquoise and gold.

With that I slipped the stone into my pocket and turned my attention to finding my way back. I hoped Esther hadn't woken up and been worried.

Miraculously I managed to find the way quite easily. But as I was about to enter the clearing - just momentarily out of the corner of my eye - I caught a glimpse of something utterly disturbing. So disturbing I almost burst into tears.

Not wanting to believe my eyes, I checked again, but this only revealed what I had feared. For standing in the darkness, about five meters to my left, I could make out a very tall and extremely powerful figure. In less than a heartbeat, all my senses became super-alert, and despite the night heat, I suddenly felt freezing cold. Even in practically no light I could tell the shadowy figure was unclothed and possibly as jet-black as a Howler monkey.

A very potent survival mechanism we all possess, practically from birth, is the ability to instantaneously recognise our own species. And that was the problem; I didn't recognise what I had just seen standing there. Instead I had the overwhelming sense that it wasn't human, despite it being very upright on two legs. There was something so strange about its stature, and its energy -it seemed to emit a totally unfamiliar resonance. Something told me this wasn't a man, beast or anything of that nature.

I switched off the torch and stood in total darkness waiting for it to move, my mind stumbling to get a grip. I didn't want to draw its attention to the shack and possibly put Esther in danger too. But what danger, I had no idea what this thing was? Trying to rationalise what I'd just seen, I asked myself if it could be an alien, but quickly dismissed the thought.

My mind then journeyed to tales of forest creatures or shadow beings described in certain shamanic traditions, folk law and mythologies. It didn't help. I had encountered different entities in dreams and visions, but never in normal waking consciousness. Moreover this figure carried a totally corporeal energy - I could actually feel its breath and muscular physicality hanging in the air.

Still no movement, I looked over. I now found it almost impossible to visually locate the creature without the tiny drizzle of light from the torch. In complete darkness and being eaten alive by mosquitoes, I began to convince myself that I was tired and imagining the whole thing, but my instincts told me different. Could it be a long denied part of my psyche finally reasserting itself? A blinding array of strange and diverse possibilities flashed across my imagination. Again I could feel my inner knowing refusing these attempts at deflection.

Finally, drained of vitality and the will to conjure any more imaginings, I simply started to cry. There was nothing else to be done. The past few months had stripped away all the armored plating I normally created to shield myself from life. Perhaps this was my way of releasing all the unhappiness. I just didn't know.

Force ripped through my body and now I was sobbing uncontrollably. After all the relentless dreams, visions and imaginings, sobbing seemed the only solution. There was no power in the world that could argue against it.

As tears streamed down my face I was gripped by an intense desire to connect with the shadow creature. I stared in its direction. But something very mysterious happened. My eyes couldn't fix on anything yet I knew beyond doubt that I was being smiled at. I stood defenseless, feeling that smile beaming right through the forest and deep into my soul.

My heart burst open. Suddenly I felt like I'd just caught sight of an angel instead of a demon. It was the strangest thing and all I could do was bask in that perceived smile. Right then I became life's destination, I was dissolving into the elixir of that smile; invisible geometry putting everything back into place.

After a while – I really have no idea how long – I sensed the smile disengage and disappear back into the forest. It was very soft and effortless. An innocent thought drifted into my mind that this could be the power of a smile given for no other reason than pure delight. Had I just seen something that is obvious and yet never seen? But even as this thought arose, I couldn't see it…

There was a beautiful glow of daylight gliding across the forest. Suddenly struck by how tired I was, I gently returned to the corrugated shack. Esther was sleeping peacefully. Little did I know, it would soon be her turn to have some amazing adventures and challenges of her own: it was that kind of journey and those stories are for her to tell.

Later that morning I traced the spot where I thought the shadow creature had been, looking for prints, some evidence of its existence. Nothing. The only sign that something special had taken place was that I no longer had a single mosquito bite, scratch or sting on my body.

In the cleansing brightness of the morning sun we sat watching children play and people slowly going about their business. The village hummed with life.

I watched this great teacher: life moving itself to where it needed to go. Reaching into my pocket I took out the turquoise and gold flexed stone. It now looked like a miniature earth balanced in the palm of my hand.......

I finished leafing through the old traveling sketchbook. I turned back to the words written on that magical day as the turquoise and gold stone shone in the palm of my hand.

Shadows are filled with light.

No matter what we may think, Nature decides exactly the right moment for us to come home to our own radiance. Nature decides where the moments of seeing will occur and how much of Her great mystery She will reveal. Only when She is ready will we behold the wonder waiting to be discovered in our blood, in our minds and in the world. Like the magical yarn paintings of the Huichol Indians, our stories are woven in many different colors and threads; yet the same hand weaves them all. Only when the time is right and we are ripe, will every experience be seen as the after-glow of the freedom it came from.

At thirty-three, afraid and exhausted in the dark forest, I caught a glimpse of the utter joy of existence which sits patiently waiting for us. Only when the nightmares I projected into the darkness totally disintegrated could the smile of life be directly experienced. Suddenly shadows were filled with light. More than ten years later, in a very different forest, life once again revealed its spectacular truth. This time as all the nightmares in my mind collapsed, Life finally released me directly into its dynamic flow. And from where I now see, it is perfectly clear that nothing – not even a single breath – was ever out of place. Everything in the vast multiplicity of existence is like this.

Pointers & Reminders

GIFTING LIFE BACK TO OURSELVES

Although we cannot force the truth upon ourselves, it appears that a willingness to no longer reject one experience in favor of another loosens the tangled knots of the mind. As I mention earlier, when we accept what we have become as a result of believing that thoughts are reality, a process is ignited. I call this process **'Gifting Life Back to Ourselves'**. We offer the pain that appears to inhabit our minds and bodies back to Nature – the power that grants and accepts everything. An Intelligence far greater than ourselves. That willingness starts to bring us back to life as we glimpse our true nature and radiance without pain. Finally the uncomfortable and fearful character created by the mind can safely hand itself back to The Guiding Principle, the Absolute.

Nature unconditionally accepts every part of us. So as we gift back everything that is seemingly punishing us, with only the desire to know our truth, the mind steadily becomes calm and falls into the service of The Guiding Principle. This process gives birth to our non-fragmented self and the potential to live life free of turmoil and confusion. We discover a life filled with the most intimate and immediate connection to its own richness and diversity. I invite you to reflect on **Pointer 1 - 'soften to life'**.

DESIRE TO TOUCH THE WONDER

Another key factor in opening to The Guiding Principle is your desire to touch the wonder that moves and shapes life - a desire to know the Intelligence that orchestrates your life. This shifts your focus away from dissatisfaction and problems, towards the astonishing quality of experience itself: the solution. Your own unique experience right this moment is the only place where freedom can be found. Your immediate experience contains the answer you are searching for. I come back to this point again and again. There is no greater teacher that can facilitate freedom than Nature Herself. You are Nature and can be nothing else.

The reason why we miss The Guiding Principle is not because it is too complicated, but because it is so simple.

Remember you don't need any special knowledge or ability to sense The Guiding Principle's signal. Remember to use the potent messengers of **'Aliveness'**, **'Creativity'**, **'Beauty'**, and **'Intelligence'** as your guides.

Remain open to the possibility that the qualities that attract you to something are not intrinsic to the thing in and of itself, but rather are messengers that transmit the very essence of Presence. All phenomena are impermanent, only the message they deliver is permanent.

*You are the Aliveness in everything that
appears as aliveness.*

*You are the Creativity in everything that
appears creative.*

*You are the Beauty in everything that
appears to be beautiful.*

*You are the Intelligence in every mind,
heart and body.*

Another way to put this is, the wonder is already touching you.

Allow yourself to *feel your way into life* instead of constantly *thinking life*. Notice how Nature is constantly speaking to you and through you, touching and moving you on so many different levels: sound, sensations, silence and the aromatic essences of life.

The mind is clearly seen as a miracle once we no longer believe it has the power to control anything or manifest anything. And a mind that sees that The Guiding Principle is the loving touch of Life, no longer seeks to make enemies of thoughts. It knows they are never personal. The stories that appear in our minds are Nature weaving Her patterns.

Everything is constantly pointing to your own amazing non-separate identity without need of adjustment or censorship. Very importantly every human being has his or her own unique journey. Wherever you are and whatever your circumstances, these are the raw materials of your liberation. Every conceivable circumstance is infused with the seeds of Grace. There is no more war in a mind that recognises this.

THE INFINITE TREASURE OF SURPRISES

The Guiding Principle contains no energy, needs no purpose and seeks no meaning, yet it appears to have one unquestionable characteristic which is **surprise**! In the tropical forest I followed the symbols contained in the dreams and eventually discovered a treasure. Only it wasn't made of turquoise and gold. The treasure was something completely unexpected.

My journey through Mexico and Guatemala demonstrates how Nature delivers her revelations in the unexpected. I trust you got a sense of this because it's exactly how The Guiding Principle shows us the way. *The Guiding Principle is an infinite treasure of surprises*. And to become intimately involved, intimately fascinated with life, is an invitation to be surprised. It is an invitation to touch the wonder as it flows through your being.

Bring your attention to where your life is not doing what you expected. Look closely and ask what empowering and exciting actions you are being guided to take. Instead of solely focusing on your thoughts, discover what your whole being wants to communicate.

CLOSER TO ANGELS

All of the ideas, openings and pointers I share in this book are an invitation to be surprised. Don't simply believe that anything I say is true, test everything directly through your own experience and uncover the truth for yourself.

At a certain point in life – it doesn't matter when - we must all without exception, surrender the belief that we can control life. We never are in control of anything and the dropping away of this idea only leaves The Guiding Principle resplendent in all its glory. We see how incredible and liberating it is not to be Master of the Universe. Beliefs no longer get in the way of the joy pouring from every single experience. Dal captured the essence of this when he said, *"When you think you're the one moving your life, the beauty of life is always invisible."*

We are only separate from Nature in the mysterious flux of our minds. It is possible to see that we are closer to Angels than we could ever have imagined. We are nebulous beings made of light, endlessly arising out of pure love.

When it is seen that the very experience that you are having right now is effortlessly and unconditionally given, there is no need to force anything. And when this understanding happens, the mind flows, the body flows, the world flows.

The next thought that comes is
The Guiding principle.

The next feeling is
The Guiding Principle.

The desire to change, to live in a different way is
The Guiding Principle.

The next action you take is
The Guiding Principle.

The words that you have just read are
The Guiding Principle.

One simple truth that reveals the miracle of your life.

ADDENDUM

THE ADVENTURE CONTINUES

LIVING POWERFULLY

Those with power have no power.

It sounds like a complete contradiction, but let me explain.

How can we walk this world with power, not the sorry excuse for power that we are sold by our current culture?

Power is found when you connect with your own true nature: living with truth and passion right by your side. Living with the possibility of failure and disappointment right by your side.

True power is when you have nothing to hide, when nothing is your enemy because you see clearly that everything that appears in this world is in fact inviting you to recognise your greatest truth.

This doesn't mean that you are undefended; instead it means that you are in fact invincible. Living your truth in each moment with an open heart – the willingness to venture into the shadows with an open heart – is the life-giving meaning of power.

To walk this world with power means that you know - not intellectually - but you know, from the deepest part of your being, that you possess no power of your own.

You can start by surrendering all your perceived power to the Great Mystery of life – to Nature. This is simply a catalyst. At first it will be almost impossible to surrender anything. However, if you persist with this as a **creative act** – something that calls for you to be imaginative and experimental in how you actually surrender - it will gradually become easier.

For example, you can use art (no artistic skill needed, this is only for you), drawing or creating some form of visual representation of power you feel you have to own, display or exert over others.

Once it is out of your head and on paper or in another form just tear it up or dismantle it. Experiment and see what happens. Make up another way to surrender that doesn't involve you sitting and trying to force yourself to surrender anything.

Importantly it doesn't need to feel as if it's working. By linking this to creativity, the process is opened out, and to your surprise you will begin to feel the act of surrendering being taken out of your hands: the creative energy or aspect of Life will take over. It will be tangible.

You will know that your nature and everything that appears in your experience is granted life through 'Grace'.

When you have no power – when you have surrendered your power over to Nature, Life, Presence or the good of all – you step into the wonderful paradox: you become powerful.

You see that there is never anything to lose or gain in this manifest world. You fall in love with this world with all its sadness and pain.

You are no longer afraid of those who appear to want to destroy you: you fall in love with your own death. You die to the old, separate self - the little god that lives in your head. Life deepens and deepens as you increasingly live immersed in the miraculous connection, The Guiding Principle of all things manifest and unmanifest.

To live this way is a complete adventure. I'm not for one second saying it's easy. It is raw, visceral, challenging and compelling. Life is felt without a filter: anything is possible: anything can be created. This is freedom.

Once you have tasted the delicious possibility of freedom, there is no longer any choice. You are an instrument played by Life for no reason, improvised moment to moment to moment.

To stay in the conversation visit:

www.TheGuidingPrinciple.com

Lightning Source UK Ltd.
Milton Keynes UK
UKOW04f2129230913

217779UK00003B/734/P